RAGS TO
RICHES

HOW BEAUTY ICONS
MADE IT BIG

This book is dedicated to Jim, Taylor, and Payton, my loving family. I want my daughters to dream big, swing big, and live big. I want them to know anything is possible and to follow their passions!

FOREWORD

The beauty industry is my first love and my passion! I jumped into it in 1982, and I was immediately head over heels for the opportunity, creativity, and energy of the industry. I showed up at my first job Shears and Sears (don't laugh I didn't know better) and thought my clientele would be handed to me. Boy was I wrong! I soon realized that I didn't understand the business of beauty, as I hadn't been taught that in school. School focuses on passing the board exams. 15% of our financial success is our technical ability the other 85% is Sales, Marketing, Operations, and finance. I was a good technician but knew nothing about the business of beauty.

When I found myself divorced with two young daughters, I had to focus on making money, rather than building my business. I was determined to make it work, even when my community told me to get a "real" job. After a long and difficult process, I am now almost 40 years into this industry, and I can honestly say that it has given me LIFE.

I built a solo business of $250,000 as a technician and built a multimillion-dollar salon/ spa. Our salon was the top 1% in the nation and the top 10% in the world. I have been able to travel the world, and have written best-selling books and spoken all over the world, helping salon and spa owners to build profitable businesses. This has now become my true passion.

This book takes all our collective experiences and gives it to you, the reader, on a journey from doing it wrong to doing it right. This anthology is the book I wish I'd had as a young technician – to be inspired by the giants and see how the new generation is monetizing their gifts and talents. Our hope is that you are inspired, motivated, and, more importantly, equipped with the tools to create your own million-dollar legacy.

I love this industry because we are creators! It took me years to realize that money is creative, and we are masters at creativity. I know that if I can do it, you can do it. I know that the stories in this book will be the light that you need to find your way to an amazing career. This industry has so much to offer; you just have to believe and be in radical action toward your future! I can't wait to see what you create on your own journey. I know mine has been unrecognizable and unbelievable!

Do the work in this book, follow the leaders on social media to stay inspired – each one of the authors is an unsung hero. It is now your job to create a path for the next generation and be the change you wish to see in the world. Make this industry a better industry because you were in it! We believe in you. I believe in you.

I am your sister in the journey. Tag me so I can follow you on your quest for greatness! Remember, wealth is your birthright!

Susie Carder
Profit Coach
www.susiecarder.com

Table of Contents

INTRODUCTION

First of all: who am I, and why am I writing this book? As the owner and founder of the ever-growing Luxe Salon Spa and Laser Center, I believe it is time for me to share the lessons and gems that got me to where I am today. I wasn't always a business owner, or even working in the beauty industry. Coming from the finance world and a successful accounting career, I took the leap into the world of beauty in 2005. This was not really ever something I envisioned myself doing before, but it was the best decision I made. Looking back, it was probably the core belief that my father instilled in me that fueled my drive to make this move. He always used to tell me, "You can have anything you want in your lifetime; all you have to do is work for it!" After graduating with an accounting degree, I soon realized that CPA firms and Fortune 500 companies weren't really for me. This was clear to me once I got married. I made the initial decision that got me to where I am today: I want to be a stay-at-home mom that worked for myself so I could have flexibility in my schedule. Working for myself was my best bet. I would be in control of my schedule and money.

It was then that I decided to get my electrolysis and esthetics license, and ended up making six figures out of my house by only working two and half days a week! I don't know whether you are working from home right now as you read this book, or whether being your own boss is something you want to do, but being able to accomplish that was the biggest game-changer in my life. I grew my business in such a way that I could no longer work out of my house, and I knew that I needed to move the business from my house to rented space. After searching for the perfect space, I ended up buying a small spa that felt like a good fit. However, it turned out to be headed toward bankruptcy. Thank goodness I only bought the assets. After six months of being open, I was able to reinvest my profits, which enabled me to purchase additional space. Thus, increasing the services offered to include all salon services I offer today. Shortly after, I purchased one of the first laser hair removal machines in Rochester. That step really took my business to the next level with the influx of new clients. I outgrew the space I was in and again, in search of another location with more space. I was able to find a 16,000 square foot building, which I purchased. Currently, 9,000 square feet is now home to the Luxe Salon Spa and Laser center.

This brings me to *why* I wanted to write this book. With all this success, I felt it was time for me to share all the tips and tricks that got me to where I am today. After I had moved my business to a new location in 2012, I decided to take several courses with *Empowering You Consulting,* which started my consulting career. This opened up the doors to becoming a consultant for salons and spas throughout the United States. My vision was to give back to those who want to be savvy business owners and be empowering leaders within their domain. There were just so many lessons that I wanted to share, but I never attempted to turn them into a book until now. That was until the pandemic hit and the beauty industry was dimming. I took a *Global Leadership Program* course with Susie Carder, which is much more extensive than any MBA program, which excels entrepreneurs to the next level. This experience gave me the knowledge and resources to write this book.

Reading this book is an excellent start and will undoubtedly put you on the right track to success! Amplify your steps by finding local salons/spas that offer training programs and submerge yourself in an environment that supports your venture in learning and growing. Hire a coach that will help you put all of the necessary procedures and systems in place so you are not wasting money and a great deal of time. This will save you thousands of dollars in the long run! Understand that this process is not going to happen overnight. If you already have a job, keep working on yourself and your finances. The right time to transition from behind the chair to owning a salon or spa is simply and plainly when the numbers and your finances allow it. Write out a detailed business plan and know what you need to work on and what systems need to be put in place in order for you to take a step back from behind the chair, or out of the esthetic's room. This is one reason why salons/spas were the second type of business to close, right behind restaurants, during the pandemic. This was because of the lack of preparation and a solid business model.

For now, pay very close attention to the lessons and assessments of this book. My journey to making the transition from working as a technician to working more on the business started out by really knowing what my end game was. I knew that I wanted to work on the business, not in the business and that I wanted to own a salon/spa with fifty plus employees. I realized the only way to grow the business was to work on the business. I knew I wanted to increase the average number of service and retail sales. So, I set goals for my finances, marketing, and social media.

It is my goal that, by the time you finish reading this book, you will have been guided through personal and professional success and, as a result, you will begin to see your life and profits grow, and your potential reached! Each chapter covers a different beauty icon that has made it big in all areas of the beauty industry. I cherry-picked these people, searching for the best icon's stories of how they made it huge, their highs and their lows, and defining moments based on the topic of the chapter. After reading through their story, we will go into an assessment based on the topic, and bring it back to the need-to-know business smarts. It is my suggestion that as you read the book, stop and think of where YOU are in your life and where you want to end up. Write this down and do the assessment at the end of each chapter.

Make notes of what your biggest takeaways are from each chapter and the action steps that YOU need to take.

For the chapter assessments, make sure that your answers to the questions are on a scale of 1 to 10. The assessments are to show you where you currently are, compared to where you want to be. After completing each chapter's assessment, take some time and write down two to three things from each that you will focus on, and work towards starting. Let the journey begin!

CHAPTER 1:
SKILLS TO PAY THE BILLS

Drew Schaefering

Drew grew up in St. Louis, Missouri. Although he was always particular about his aesthetic, he never got fancy haircuts at expensive salons. Actually, Drew started styling his own hair in *kindergarten*. Drew had a family friend whom he would visit once a month. "I would watch what he did. I would always think to myself, *I can do this better than a lot of other people who are doing it,*" he said. As he got older, he started cutting his own hair, his friend's hair, and even his teacher's hair in high school. His friends would compliment his hair and ask him who did it; his response was that he sat in the mirror and did it himself. When he went to college, the trend continued; he was cutting his hair, his professor's hair, and even his teammate's hair. Drew went to college at Charleston Southern University and Gardner Webb University on a soccer scholarship. As a Division 1 (D1) soccer player, he was always determined to be the hardest worker. Along with playing a sport, Drew was on his way to earning a degree in finance. When it was time for him to graduate, Drew had to make a decision between going into finance or taking a chance on this "creative endeavor." He truly felt like it was time for him to grow up and take the first step toward adulthood. Drew had an opportunity to take a "big boy job" in the finance industry.

Drew's father, on the other hand, thought that his son should follow his true passion for doing hair. "Don't take that job. You have something unique and different. Try hair school; if you don't like it, that job will always be there," his dad said. Taking his father's advice into consideration, Drew signed up for hair school. After the first day, he realized that was his true passion. He was really dedicated and had a great work ethic that came from being an athlete.

After hair school, Drew took a job at a family friend's salon. Every salon in St. Louis wanted him to work for them because of how talented he was. The family friend owned an upscale salon, even though it was small. The salon owner told Drew if he worked there, he would teach him everything he needed to know in order to grow. The salon owner also recognized that Drew had something special. People were surprised that he worked at a small salon instead of a big, sexy salon. Drew started by watching his mentor; at this point, he was "learning through osmosis." Six months into his apprenticeship, Drew was taking advanced academy courses. Drew and the salon owner would travel to New York and train for the weekend with L'OREAL Professionnel. "A couple of times, both the lead educator and their assistants came up to me and said, 'Hey, how long have you been doing hair? Have you ever thought about working with a brand?'," he said. He didn't really know what that meant.

Growing up as an athlete, Drew thought this meant that he would be sponsored by the brand and receive free things. He didn't understand what "working with a brand" in the hair industry meant. His mentor knew he was ready and asked Drew if he thought he was ready. Drew replied that he didn't think so, but he was going to take a chance. As we know, Drew was (and still is) determined as hell. He was flown to New York for an in-person audition and made the L'OREAL Professionnel team. "They saw a great deal of potential. They knew I was young and they wanted to help me grow, knowing I would help them in the future," he commented. After he made the team, they fast-tracked him. Pretty soon, he was traveling every weekend to attend different training sessions to shadow hairstylists and learn more about the industry. Drew's clientele in St. Louis quickly grew. Within eight months, he was fully booked and was booking three months out.

He traveled for training and did hair in St. Louis for about three years. He loved the educational aspect. During this period, Drew's friend asked him to come to New York to work fashion week. Drew replied, "Sure, but I don't know what that is." He didn't know at the time that he would be part of a team made up of the most talented hairstylists in the world. He became part of this team by sneaking backstage. "I'm that person," he would say, pointing to a name on the list. At the time, they weren't checking IDs or anything. Even though some would say this was slightly morally wrong, one of the French hairstylists admired Drew's ambition and motivation.

Drew realized he either had to open up a salon in St. Louis to grow, or move to New York. Drew decided to move to New York. He started at a salon where he was doing a lot of educational work. He was flying back to St. Louis every four weeks to do four days of clients in order to make money. Soon, he was doing more editorial work — assisting more people and working on photoshoots. For approximately six years, he didn't work in a salon. He was just doing education, fashion stuff, and working with private clients. Drew always knew that he wanted to find a way to make passive income. After three years of living in New York, Drew came to a realization. "When you're in front of an audience, that audience wants to bring a piece of you home with them. They want to keep connecting," he noted.

He saw an opportunity to start something new: a tool company. With his business background, he knew that he had the skills and determination to create a brand with meaning. He started selling small tools such as: scissors, hair clips, combs, and tool cases. Drew didn't want the brand to be named after him. He wanted it to grow well past him. He named it **Cruxe**. In between travel, clients, and fashion work, he was working on his brand. Some days, Drew would think, *is the juice really worth the squeeze?* Even though he got discouraged sometimes, Drew really believed that *success is doing the right things consistently.* He started Cruxe because he saw an opportunity, but he also noticed that the artistic side of this industry needed some emotion behind it.

Today, Drew lives in Brooklyn, New York and works at a salon two days a week, which he started doing during the pandemic when his other work slowed down almost completely. Drew also travels a couple times a month for L'OREAL Professionnel and hosts classes for his company which he loves.

One of his biggest challenges is being spread too thin. Drew understood that managing multiple things involves a great deal of patience. He learned things take time, and he had to nurture them in order for them to grow. He believes an important part of starting new projects is making sure that you have the right people around you that will help you grow and learn through the process. You need a support system that you believe in and trust.

During my interview with Drew, I asked him "What moment in your career made you feel like you really made it?" Drew replied, "I don't feel like I have really made it yet." He believes that some people feel like they have made it and that they deserve everything and should be given everything, but that is not him. He said, "Yes I have worked my ass off. Yes, I have achieved a lot of things. Many people look at me and say, wow, if I could only be like that." Drew attributes his work ethic and determination to his time as a student athlete. "If you weren't training as hard as the person next to you, they were going to catch up," Drew comments. Even though Drew has worked with huge names like Victoria Beckham and Kim Kardashian, he doesn't feel like he has reached the peak of this mountain top in order to reach the next high point in his career. He is currently working on several projects and learning how to scale them. It's hard for Drew to feel like he has actually made it, regardless of his current accomplishments because he wants to do so many things with his career.

His biggest hurdle so far was fear. It was something he had to overcome. He feels fear can be a motivator, but we have to get over the fear of failure — fear of not being good enough or being successful — and just try it anyway. Another hurdle he mentioned was when he moved to New York. He wanted to find a salon he could feel secure at. He wanted to find a salon that would allow him to travel back to St. Louis so that he had financial security. Everyone told him he was crazy, and that no salon would let him do that. Hearing other people's doubts only gave Drew more motivation to look for a salon that would give him this flexibility. Whenever someone said that one of his new business ventures will be hard to accomplish, he accepted the challenge and faced it head on. "Those are the two major hurdles, but it's also having the discipline to keep moving forward," Drew said. Finding your own path, staying true to it, while simultaneously balancing friendships and relationships is no easy task.

Advice is something that everyone searches for, whether it's from your friends, parents, or mentor. Drew says that the best advice and the worst advice he received were one in the same. "I've had a lot of people tell me to do what other people, who are already successful, are doing," Drew said. On social media, for instance, Drew doesn't post the same type of content that everyone else posts. His content is visibly more edgy and alternative than most of the content that we see on a daily basis. Drew does not like to "follow the wave;" he wants to create his own wave. "We don't need more copies of copies. There's no authenticity in doing that. For me, that has to be number 1; authenticity in everything I'm doing," Drew said.

Drew is unapologetically humble. While working with top names in the industry, he realizes they are people first. Even when he has "pinch me" moments that make him stop and think about where he is today, he still reminds himself they're just "people." He has worked with celebrities like Eva Longoria and Tilda Swinton, to name a few. These top celebrities are still just human beings, and you have to treat them as such.

Since Drew is a businessman *and* an artist, he has some advice for people looking to start their own business. First of all, he recommends that you know your long-term goals and systems for what you are trying to accomplish. As a creator, Drew enjoys living in the moment; however, this doesn't disregard the fact that having a plan is a necessary component of success. "If it doesn't make dollars it doesn't make cents [sense]," he notes. Creating one, three, and five year plans helps Drew stay focused. This doesn't mean that you can't stop and walk through other doors that are opening, but it prevents you from just wandering aimlessly through life. For his second piece of advice, he emphasized the importance of having a mentor. Finding successful people that you respect can help you learn to navigate the industry. You don't always have to like them, but you should find people who are going to challenge you. When finding new people to learn from, it is important that they don't just boost your ego. When people agree with you, it makes you happy, but it doesn't help you learn. You need to find people who will question you and ultimately, educate you on how to be successful. His third piece of advice is that money management is an important component to success. Learning how to set your money aside and invest for the future is extremely important as an artist. You have to treat your whole life like a business, because if you don't, then you will have no one else to do it for you. A final piece of advice that Drew offered, and arguably the most important, was to be realistic with your finances and live within your means. Having fun is an important part of life, but we need to be realistic in the way that we spend our money. When people decide that they want to start a business, they forget about everything else that it takes to run a company. Running a business is different from running *your business* behind the chair. Drew consults and mentors people so they can learn to navigate the industry. When they come to him and explain that they want to start a business, they are only thinking about the shiny and fun part of owning a business, not the difficulties that can arise. Social media has made it easier for us to feel like there is only happiness in running a business, so no one sees the digging in the dirt that it takes to get a business off of the ground. When people have the motivation to go forward and start something new, that's great, but they shouldn't go for it blindly. Don't go into it thinking that it's all roses and sunshine. Go into it with a business plan, with mentors, and with a team of people around you.

Making small adjustments can help your business in the long run. Drew decided that instead of doing a complete overhaul of his businesses, he was going to keep making these little changes to refine them. He wanted to continue doing fashion, editorial, and educational work because he loved these things. Drew's three to five year goal is to enjoy the fruits of these little adjustments he is making in his life. He wants to do these things at a greater volume with more efficiency. Defining the small changes to be made is a task that requires focus and motivation — two things that Drew had a great deal of practice with during his time as a student athlete. His ultimate goal with his hair company is to be the most unique; he wants to be able to do things that other larger companies can't do because they are so big that it would take a much longer time to adjust.

Drew's biggest influence in his life is his father. He encouraged Drew to attend hair school, supported Drew through every new venture, and is part-owner of the Cruxe brand. Another major influence in Drew's life is the family friend who owned the first salon that Drew worked at. He gave Drew space to grow and the knowledge to continue working toward his dreams. Drew is also grateful for the several hairstylists who helped him along his journey and took him under their wings. They gave him opportunities and taught him responsibility. Even though they "threw him into the deep end," they made him aware of what was in the water before he was thrown in to fend for himself. When he had the support of people who had done it and who believed in him, it gave him that much more confidence.

I asked Drew if any experience stuck out in his mind; he shared a story about a hairshow he worked on. This event happened early on in Drew's career. L'OREAL Professionnel was launching the first non-ammoniated permanent color and the team was doing a hair show at the Intercoiffure. Drew had done multiple hair shows before, but this was the most elite platform he had encountered. There were multiple models who wore intricate headpieces that would be applied in chunks by different stylists, as the models traveled through an assembly line. Drew was applying a section of the headpiece before the show and as he put one of the bobby pins in, the model flinched. He asked the model if she was okay and she replied saying she was fine. The show continued normally and the models would dance and travel to the next stylist to have a part of the hairpiece removed. When Drew's model got to the last hairstylist, he removed the pin from her hair and blood started running down her face. Everyone in the front row was throwing napkins at her to stop the bleeding. Eventually, the stylist realized what was happening and started wiping at her forehead to try and "save face." Drew said that he was horrified by what happened. Within his first few years in the industry, he had made someone bleed in front of 2,000 people. Drew has done her hair multiple times since this incident and says that he will never make her pay when she sits in his chair.

Drew's advice is to try everything and follow your gut instinct. Find a way to make things happen, but don't do it blindly. It's important to try new things, but it is also important to understand what it takes to be successful in any business venture you tackle. Mentors play a significant role because they have been through it and can give you some tips on what to do/what not to do. A recurring theme in this book is emphasizing that **we really don't know**

what we don't know, so having the right mentor along the way is a sure solution to this problem. A lot of people look at Drew today and think he's crazy. Drew says that he is more like a well-tuned swiss army knife because he tries everything. A lot of the wildly successful people are sniper rifles; they are one-job people and they do it extremely well. If you know what you want, focus on that and do whatever you can do to make it work. If you are interested in many different things, then try them all.

As a multimillion-dollar salon & spa owner and beauty expert, I've spent 20 years building my financial wealth in this industry. I love this industry because, like Drew, we get to write our own tickets! There is so much knowledge and opportunity all around you, first as a technician and then as a salon owner.

The assessment for this chapter is outlined below. Go through it now, and I will explain more after. Rate yourself on a scale of 1-10: 1 being the worst, 10 being you nailed it, and 5 if you are in the middle. (Be as honest as possible!)

1. **Do you have your service goals for the year and have them broken down by month, week, and day?**
2. **Do you have your retail goals for the year and have them broken down by month, week, and day goals?**
3. **Do you know your average retail ticket, and do you track it?**
4. **Do you know your average service ticket, and do you track it?**
5. **If you have a team, do you meet with them at least once a month to coach them on meeting their service and retail goals?**
6. **Do you have a loyalty program, and do you track it?**
7. **Do you have a client database?**
8. **Do you utilize social media marketing?**
9. **Do you know what your rebook rate is and for each employee if you have them?**

10. Do you have a procedure in place for clients who did not rebook the day of their last appointment?

Now that you have the numbers for each question, add them up. What is your score? The closer to 100 you are, the better you are doing. My guess is most people are under 50! Keep this note aside for references as we continue.

There are five ways you can use your skills to pay the bills. These are outlined below.

1. Increase your average service ticket and retail ticket.
    a. Set goals every day and week for your service sales and retail sales.
    b. An owner or manager should meet with the team members weekly to help them achieve their goals such as: increasing their service and retail sales, coaching them so they are confident when asking clients to rebook and selling retail to clients. The owner/manager should help the technicians map out their career path, and supply them with the right tools to further their careers.
2. Plan a referral program to encourage clients' loyalty.
3. Make sure you are building your database, and your social platform to leverage your expertise and showcase your talent.
4. Continue with your business and technical education because *the more you learn, the more you EARN! You just don't know what you don't know!*
5. Stay on top of your rebooking strategies and follow-up strategies. Don't leave money on the table.

Understanding these five ideas is important, but what is more important is taking the action steps to pay the bills. Pick three of the five strategies above to implement in the next 30 days. Post on social media in the *Rags to Riches* Facebook group about what you have learned and what you will do to take it to the next level! Hair styling is a weird job. It's not cute to doubt yourself. Not only is it not charming at all, but it serves absolutely zero purposes. Blind confidence in yourself sounds bizarre, but in pretty much any line of work, you need to have the confidence to lead yourself to the next big thing. You need to start taking baby steps and keep moving forward. It all comes down to this: **if you're not willing to go for it, you may miss conquering your dream career.**

CHAPTER 2:
SWING BIG, DREAM BIG

Aika Flores

"Just trust me, and I will prove you wrong."

Aika Flores, a Los Angeles-based hairstylist and celebrity men's groomer, has defeated all odds to reach where she is as a salon owner specializing in both classic and experimental looks. Born in the Philippines, raised in Las Vegas, and a Los Angeles resident for the last nine years, she's made a name for herself through hard work and determination. She received her Cosmetology license from Vidal Sassoon Academy. She went on to assist and work at a salon on Melrose Avenue for three years before transitioning to celebrity assisting and grooming under a mentor. Born and raised in a Filipino family household, speaking out about her passion for hairstyling was not easy. Her family was weary about her reaching her dreams. Her parents, like many traditional Filipino families, had always encouraged her to pursue a career in the medical field. Aika's parents overcame a lot of obstacles themselves to get to Las Vegas from the Philippines, so they really just wanted what was best for Aika, which was to live a financially stable and successful life. Her parents wanted what all other parents wanted for their kids.

For Aika, what was "best" for her wasn't becoming a nurse or any other medical professional. Her grandma was the first person who exposed her to the world of hairstyling. Watching her grandma work with hair gave Aika that spark of excitement that she simply couldn't put into words. The problem with people not taking hairstyling as a serious profession is that there is an abundance of affordable salons with hair stylists that do not get paid enough to grow their income. Aika was determined! The first step of taking matters into her own hands was to drop out of college for nursing, move to Los Angeles, and figure out how she was going to get into the career path of her dreams. Not too many people have the guts to make a jump as big as Aika's. I have to applaud her confidence!

Aika has two main life values that she acts on every single day. One of them is to *just listen to yourself*. Moving to Los Angeles was probably the boldest step she had ever taken, up to this point in her life. Today Aika's drive to take risks is so strong that she no longer asks "what if there's just a sack of potatoes on the other side of the door?" Instead, she asks: "WHO CARES what is on the other side, and even if it is just a sack of potatoes, what is on the OTHER side of the potatoes?" Sounds simple, but it's actually an extremely powerful mindset to have and one that got Aika to where she is today! She transitioned from set and print to men's grooming in 2019, having the pleasure of working with huge names in the music world and on movie sets. In addition to personal grooming, Aika has also groomed talent for *Man About Town UK*, *The Time UK*, and NUDE Magazines. In her time off set, Aika operates out of her own private studio in Beverly Hills under the name "Project".

Her confidence in her gut instincts began to solidify by the time she was fresh out of hairstyling school. Little did she know that she had not even begun to understand the industry. That's when she came up with her second life value. It was so important to her that she now considers it her motto: *never stop learning*. Aika emphasizes that the moment you stop learning is the moment you become stagnant. If you're lucky enough to have someone come up to you and say, "Hey, I want to show you something," and your first thought is *Oh, I already know that*, then you simply don't quite get it. Everyone is knowledgeable in different ways and has different ways of viewing things. If you just allow yourself to listen, then you will be able to gain valuable knowledge from every single conversation you have.

Aika's first stepping stone was her apprenticeship working at a salon in Los Angeles. Working for someone who values education so much was why Aika decided to take her first step there. Little did Aika know that, even if she didn't end up working at that particular salon for very long, the opportunity of working at a salon where learning is the priority allowed her to build the necessary skills to start her own salon.

Hairstyling apprenticeship is difficult. You're on your feet for hours on end, working yourself up from free gigs to a pretty low base price. Aika spent years searching for models to do their hair for free just so she could slowly build up her reputation and clientele. Again, her determination was unstoppable! Now, the beautiful thing about Aika is that she never feels like "AHA! I've made it." It might sound a little draining to have this type of mindset because you're basically always running after another dream. But to Aika, so long as you look back at how far you've come and remind yourself that the sky's the limit, you should not allow yourself to settle. After all, if someone else can do it, so can you. And so naturally, Aika didn't want to settle and was making a living out of doing what she loves. She wanted to continue to grow and expand her services.

That's when she started to pay more attention to Instagram and social media. Her breaking point was when she worked hard for two weeks straight and felt like her paycheck simply didn't match how exhausted she was feeling. She was reaching burnout. We've all felt that way, but quitting isn't really an option for most of us. For Aika, it was time to exercise her "WHO CARES" motto and take the next leap. So, she started reaching out to male celebrity hairstylists, just to ask: "How can I be a part of helping you?" She didn't expect anyone to really respond more than just a quick "Thank You." However, one day, she got a response from a top groomer who needed an assistant for a big upcoming project. Aika kept her positive attitude and led with a helping hand. Aika didn't even think that she would be getting paid, but she was following her gut instinct to move on to the next stepping stone. Turns out, the big project was for a huge reunion tour. Aika was torn between continuing to grow her knowledge and taking the step to following her gut instinct - both were very important to her. She tried to balance the two, but eventually the inevitable came where she had to decide between growing her clientele base and committing to the reunion tour.

Aika found herself flying to different parts of the world doing what she loved. She felt like she had hit her "AHA" moment because she was basically doing exactly what she wanted: hair and not always staying behind the chair. That was until the pandemic hit. With no more trips around the world, she wasn't sure what to do. Working with this top hairstylist had allowed her to grow her clientele, who wanted to keep working with her. Aika wasn't sure how to balance the mens grooming and the occasional gigs she was offered for her pre-existing clientele. So, it was around when the pandemic hit that Aika decided that it was time to invest in opening her own studio so she could also work with her growing clientele. Traveling to people's homes to do their hair, due to closures, wasn't an option anymore because her clientele had grown too big. It's pretty clear that Aika doesn't like limitations. It was only after she started working with a friend that she realized that she didn't like working FOR someone. Once June 2020 hit, Aika was ready to continue working with men's grooming, but also balance running her own hair studio. Aika's story is no doubt putting in your mind the thought: "If she can do it, so can I. " That's why I am sharing her story, to inspire. But as Aika says, you need to be willing to learn. You can follow Aika's journey on her Instagram (@

aikafloreshair) to take a look at some of the clients she has worked with. You can also visit her portfolio at www.aikaflores.me. She is seriously BIG TIME!

For this chapter's assessment, answer the following questions on a separate piece of paper.

1. **Do you want to own your own business and have employees?**
2. **Write out your description of an ideal employee.**
3. **What is your interview process?**
4. **Do you have a written interview process so that all candidates are evaluated the same?**
5. **Do you have a clear job description stating what is expected in detail?**
6. **Do you have a written code of conduct policy?**
7. **Will you have an interviewee complete a technical interview, with a written grade sheet?**
8. **Do you have a comprehensive and written training manual?**
9. **Do you have a career plan to grow your employee's numbers and career?**
10. **Do you have a written 30, 60, or 90-day trial process to become an employee?**

As you grow your business with employees, the above ten things should be done in order to streamline your business.

My, Karen's, research comes as no surprise that 29% of salons and spas fail because they simply run out of cash. Running a salon is not cheap! Plus, it requires constant management and an efficient business model. Generally, people go into the salon business thinking that they can make money right from the start. In reality, it takes between $50,000-65,000 to get a beauty salon up and running and about 6-8 months to start making profits. Additionally, most suppliers require immediate payment (especially if you are new to the industry). Plus rent, utilities, and wages can take a toll on your income if it's not what you expected. So, you have to be incredibly organized to be able to survive the first few months without closing. But do not let this prevent you from following your dreams of owning a salon or spa. Hire a coach to help you draft a comprehensive business plan based on your aspirations. Have contingency money in case things go south, and only invest in things you consider a priority. Also, you must build a support network. According to the Small Business Administration (SBA), more often than not, businesses go bankrupt because owners believe they can do everything by themselves.

What are the biggest mistakes salon owners make?

<u>Hiring The Wrong People</u>

Like with any company, hiring the right staff can make or break your business - especially in the service industry. Surprisingly, 23% of startups fail because they did not have the right team. It is not always easy to find qualified personnel. In most cases, employees are the reason behind bad customer experiences, ultimately ruining your reputation. For instance, if you hire a hairstylist that is amazing at his/her job, but is always calling in sick, clients will eventually find another stylist, and stop coming to the salon. They also might spread the word about having a bad experience with your salon, which will bring negative reviews about your business. Thus, as a salon owner, you have to be *very* careful when selecting your team. Always ask for references, and actually call them, when recruiting new staff members as first impressions and resumes can be deceiving. It is surprising how many people do not call references in this industry! Keep in mind that deciding who not to hire is even more important than finding the right candidate. Hire slow and fire fast, and have a written hiring procedure in place. I suggest having interviewees come back for two or three interviews, and with different people. I would have them shadow for two to three hours before you make them an offer. It is important to have them meet as many people on your team as possible and trust your staff's input. This weeds out anyone who might not be a good fit for the organization. It will also prove to be a good barometer for their level of interest for the industry and your salon.

Failure To Understand The Market

Understanding the market, and consequently, your ideal client, is a crucial part of running a successful business. A staggering 42% of small to medium enterprises fail because there is no market need for their services/products. There are over 300,000 salons in the United States. Not every person with a pulse is your ideal client! You and your team need to become very specific about who your ideal client is. Your mission and vision statement can help guide you!

Pricing

As a salon owner, you need to be proactive. You should continually evaluate your offerings. By doing so, you are capable of eliminating or replacing unwanted services, cutting down on expenses, and making sure that your salon/spa remains relevant. Review the costs of services at least once a year, and always look for ways to reduce expenses. For instance, just because you have bought supplies, like waxing strips, from the same vendor for years does not mean you are getting the best price. It is important to always price shop, especially nowadays!

<u>Inadequate Planning</u>

Pricing has a great deal to do with the success of your salon. For example, If you have annual sales of $500,000 and your costs are also $500,000, you might want to take a close look at your price levels. It cannot be considered a successful business. Setting prices based on what your competitors are charging or based on what you think is fair is definitely wrong. These types of practices affect your profit margin and can ultimately bankrupt your business. Thoroughly analyze your expenses and consider reasonable profit margins before setting your prices. On average, an acceptable profit margin for beauty salons is 10%, while 15-20% is ideal.

High turnover-recruiting and employee retention are huge problems in the salon and spa industry. Equally challenging, is growing and maintaining clientele and funding your services. Consider the following when deciding to open your own salon/spa.

A. **Customer Retention**. A big problem in salon businesses is focusing more on clientele growth and not as much on maintaining the existing clientele. Making small changes such as creating a loyalty program and collecting customer feedback can help improve retention rates. You have to focus on the customer experience as much as possible. I tell my staff to pretend your next client is your partner's mother and you want to marry them! They usually laugh at me! But they treat their next client like their celebrity crush! Perfect consultation, great shampoo experience, precise cutting, and the color is a home run! The client leaves with their new products, their next appointment in the books, and a hug. My stylists sing, "Going to the chapel and we're gonna get married!"

B. **No-Shows**. One of the worst things a salon owner has to deal with is overstaffing in expectation for a certain number of customers, only to have no-shows take the place of a potential paying customer. Ideally, use an online booking system. Being able to see all the available time slots can help with making sure clients are picking what works best for them. Online booking also makes it easier to send them reminders and follow-ups. Many salons and spas have a policy that if clients cancel less than 24 hours of their appointment, they are still charged full price.

C. **Insufficient Cash Reserves.** As I mentioned earlier, a successful business isn't just making big numbers in terms of revenue, but also hitting it big with the profit margin. You should have enough cash on reserve to not only launch the business, but also bring it to profitability. This means having enough to survive any downturns, too.

D. **Incorrect Product and Service Pricing**. Pricing comes down to deciding whether you want to be that affordable option, or the expensive high-end option. Both are great options, but you have to be realistic. You can't charge the cheapest haircuts in your city while hiring the most expensive stylists and offering the most expensive products. You also can't be putting expensive prices on low-budget services. Decide your salon's target client base and price accordingly.

Having the knowledge of these strategies isn't enough, mind you. Just as Aika did, you need to enter this industry with the desire to learn, confidence in your gut instinct, and being fully aware that if you don't step in and do your job, there's always going to be someone out there who will. Aika was able to reach where she was as a fairly new salon owner herself by acting on these values. By following her passion with extreme determination, she shaped *her environment* for success. For Aika, that meant going into the industry where she was following her heart and becoming the best that she could possibly be. Aika is so down to earth, a huge powerhouse, and an inspiration to so many others!

CHAPTER 3:

WORK SMART, NOT HARD

Geno Stampora

"Wasn't I just *fabulous?*"

"Yeah! You were good."

"No, but didn't you just LOVE my stuff?"

"Yes, you did good, Geno."

One day, Geno Stampora was browsing the shops in NYC. It was right after he had given one of his educational speeches and right before one of his shows. Knowing that he had a big show coming up, he bought a one-piece black jumpsuit with a large velcro belt. He thought it was super cool! He was going to look *cool*. To add the cherry on the top, he went out to buy a pair of sneakers to match. He couldn't find any black sneakers, so he bought a pair of white ones and just spray painted them black. He wanted the awesome all-black look. Black represented strength.

The young lady laughed lightly. "Do you really think that people will take you seriously? Dressed like that?"

"*Are you kidding me?*" he exclaimed. "This is a one-piece jumpsuit from Soho. That's as cool as you can get."

"Listen, Geno, don't get me wrong. You're really good. But you just have to get out of yourself."

This was one of the earliest times Geno decided to be vulnerable. One big thing Geno and I have in common is that we care deeply about educating and making an impact. When you first start educating people, you're doing it for yourself. But later on, you realize: that if you could just reach 10 people, you would be making an impact on 10 people's lives. That's a pretty significant impact. But this young lady's words kind of stuck. After the show, Geno got a call from his friend. He asked how the show went.

"I thought it went great, but the feedback said otherwise. I don't think I want to be an educator. I don't want to do any shows." He sighed on the phone. "I just want to focus on working in the salon."

"Geno, I never thought you would be one to melt at the first sight of rain."

Geno, being ever so proud of his self-determination, was shocked to hear this. Because it was true. He was allowing himself to be held back by the first obstacle that obstructed his path to success. That's when he decided that *nothing was going to stop him. Not even himself.* If you've ever had to convince yourself to not believe what people are saying about you or to you, you can understand how liberating that feeling is. Today, Geno is not only able to say "This is who I am. This is my place. This is what I am meant to do," but he actually believes it.

But who is Geno anyways? Considered an industry expert and business guru, Geno was inducted into the North American Hairstylist Awards' coveted "Hall of Leaders," only one of 24 beauty professionals in history. Owner of two beauty academies, author of *Success Dynamics*, and a guest feature in *Modern Salon, American Salon, Salon Today, Nails, Nailpro, Dayspa, Launchpad*, and almost every salon and spa trade magazine. You can also find his articles in Glamour, Elle, The New Yorker, Washingtonian Magazine, and others. Geno is the walking representation of how far pure determination and drive can take you. He had settled for building his career as an employee at a bank before any of this and had never even considered working in the beauty industry before. One day, by accident, he was walking home from work and decided to stop by the beauty school between work and home. He had gone in with the intention of meeting the girls there, nothing more. The registrar at the time, Bill Kennedy, welcomed him.

"Geno? That's your name?"

"Yes, sir! And I am a banker."

"Geno, with a name like that you can be famous *just* for your name. Why don't you try to get into the beauty industry?"

And so, just like that, Geno signed up. Because why not? According to Geno, that was the best decision of his life. After graduating from beauty school, he went to work at a salon in New Jersey and then at his friend's salon in Virginia. That led him to open up his own salon. And then a few more. Then a big beauty spa, which was a huge deal back in 1985 when there were not many beauty spas. Soon after, he opened his own beauty schools and the rest was history. By 1989, he had committed to helping younger beauty enthusiasts grow and educate themselves. Today, Geno leads more than 50 of the largest beauty shows around the country a year and has found his true passion within the beauty industry. He has made a major contribution to the beauty industry in many ways. He has owned, managed, and worked behind the chair in his collection of salons. He has owned two beauty academies, where he also instructed. Geno has been a distributor and sales consultant to salons, a major platform artist, and has shared the stage with the world's greatest artists. As an industry expert, and speaker, Geno has consulted with many manufacturers. He has educated industry artists and salespeople all over the world. He has coached the winning teams in beauty. He has been and continues to be a keynote speaker, contributing artist, and consultant to the industry.

This is not a mainstream path. Becoming comfortable in your own skin is a life-changing feeling. Being able to say, "This is who I am. This is my place. This is what I am meant to do," is something that we all strive for. Too many young people with interest in the beauty industry limit themselves by not considering all of the possibilities. If they just believe in themselves, miracles can happen. That is not to say, however, that as soon as you decide to believe in yourself things will get better. Geno says that even when he decided to trust in his vision, there was still another voice in his head telling him that he could never do it and that he was full of crap. This was when he decided that he needed to shut down the voice inside his head that was trying to convince him not to believe in himself. In order to do that, he had to seek inspiration from outside sources.

Perhaps the most important aspect of success that Geno discusses is the ability to develop mental toughness. He says that his strong mentality was not developed in one instant, but consistently over the span of a year. This year of growth is when Geno decided to give it his all, be transparent, and jump on every opportunity that presented itself. Mental toughness is not something that can be achieved and then ignored. Geno emphasizes the need to *maintain this mental toughness,* even through difficult situations. In order to keep a tough mentality you must seek inspiration. Every. Single. Day. *"The powers of inspiration are limitless."* As Geno is passionately speaking about the importance of inspiration, he turns around and points at the photos hanging in his office.

"These are pictures of me and everyone. Me and Vidal Sassoon, me and Robert Cromean's, me and Paul Mitchell, me and Jean Paul Dejoria. I have to look at them sometimes and say *'look who you are, look what you've done.'.* Because sometimes I forget."

Geno says that the goal in seeking inspiration is to make sure that the "little you" inside your head doesn't alter your positive outlook on life. We all have this little voice in our head. It's the one that tells you not to take risks because the reward might not be worth it. The voice that says you can't do it, even before you get started. As long as you remember how far you've come and never forget who you are, the voice has no choice but to stop making noise.

In a recent interview with *Modern Salon*, Geno was asked the question: "Why do you think you are such a great educator?" He explained that although he does not have any formal education himself, he discovered that the more you learn, the more you earn, and the more impact you can have. Geno says that a lot of people want a certain lifestyle, to be successful, but they are not willing to do the work. It is a practice that needs to be integrated into your daily life. To be a master you have to constantly learn, grow, and seek.

Every entrepreneur's goal is to grow a profitable business so that they too can make an impact in people's lives, and ultimately grow their earnings. To ensure your business is scaled for growth, it is essential to create a business plan. It is your road map to success and will help you think about your future milestones to build a thriving business. I believe a major piece of advice is to follow the paths of people like Geno and encourage the technical aspects of your business. Review your business plan regularly, and continue to ask yourself, "Can I afford this?" I have had consulting clients who would spend a large amount of money on unnecessary things, such as an expensive espresso machine. This client spent $10,000 for it and then another $10,000 for the next three years trying to fix it! You should always be looking to eliminate waste; such as things you don't really need, overuse of products, and lazy employees. How you spend your finances comes down to strategy, which brings me back to my main point: work smart, spend smart, and really just make smart decisions when it comes to your business.

It can be easy to get overwhelmed, especially as you scale and grow. The more clients you get, the easier it is to find yourself burnt out trying to keep up with all of the demands that come with an increased clientele. My advice for this is to manage your time *smartly* by establishing an effective and productive routine.

Geno discusses the importance of focusing on one thing at a time. He says that he is the type of person to attempt to work on 30 things at once. He learned that this was not the most effective way to handle business. Spreading yourself too thin can lead to self criticism and burnout when you can't complete all of the tasks. Focus on one thing, do it well, and then move on to the next. The key isn't to pack your schedule with things to get done, but to find a way to manage them so that everything gets done without you feeling overwhelmed.

Let's pause for a moment and evaluate where you are. On a scale from one to ten, where do you think your confidence level is at this point? (Rate yourself on a scale of 1-10: 1 being the worst, 10 being the best.)

1. **Do you believe in yourself?**
2. **Where does your confidence level currently fall?**
3. **If you say you are going to do something, do you follow through?**
4. **Do you get sidetracked easily?**
5. **Do you hold yourself accountable, or do you drag your feet?**
6. **Do you understand what your end goal is, and how to get there?**
7. **Do you prioritize your to-do lists, while setting attainable deadlines?**
8. **Do you allow time-wasters to take up a lot of your time? Time-wasters could be social media, chatting with co-workers for too long, etc.**
9. **Are you a risk-taker?**
10. **Do you see your life in a positive light even when things aren't going your way?**

Once again, add these numbers together and see where you stand out of 100.

Circle 3-4 things you want to work on!

The following are some helpful tips, and a few time management strategies that I typically use:

1. **Create to-do lists.** I know that not everyone is a list kind of person, but physically writing down your to-dos, whether it be for the day or the week, will help keep yourself on track and accountable.

2. **Re-evaluate and prioritize.** You should constantly be asking yourself where you and your business can improve. Look at your numbers and make sure all those things are still aligning with your plan and dream. Make a to-do list based on what you want to accomplish.

3. **Set difficult, but achievable deadlines.** Hold yourself accountable. Setting deadlines for yourself is a great way to get what you need to be done. For example, when I ask a staff member to do something, I always say by when. I always want to know by what date or time the task will be done.

4. **Create a dedicated workspace, or area, with limited distractions.** Keep your workspace (whether it be an office or just a random desk) clean and clutter-free. Your workspace should be a focus zone, so try to keep distractions away. If you find yourself lurking on Instagram instead of crunching numbers, try leaving your phone out of your workspace. Think about how much time you spend on your phone each day not completing anything.

5. **Set specific time periods for yourself.** We grew up in school having different periods for different topics and that shouldn't stop now. Try categorizing your to-do list and only focusing on certain sections at once.

In the end, you must always remember to prioritize what will make you the most revenue and what is ultimately best for your business. What is even more important than starting a business is sustaining it. To start, you need to finalize your business plan, vision, and mission statements. You will need to understand CSM (Customer Service Management), which is a standard term used to describe systems and tools that are used to take care of our clients and potential clients. Implement sales systems - there are numerous options out there so you will have to find what system works best for you and your business. Finance systems will also need to be implemented such as accounting, payroll, and budgets. Financial systems are vastly important for your business as you need to know what to budget for and how to track income and expenses. Your marketing and branding are major - ask yourself who your ideal client is, how you will market yourself, website design, and tracking. Utilize social media as it is one of the top ways to market yourself and your brand; it's the best platform to find your audience. I think that one of the most essential systems to have in place when scaling your business is a financial system. Accounting and finance are the *backbones* of any business! If you don't have an understanding of your finances, you will undoubtedly be losing money and could possibly go bankrupt. My accounting and finance degrees served me well for owning my salon, spa, and laser center as well as my consulting clients. It was shocking to see the number of salon and spa owners who were astonished to realize that they were losing lots of money every month. Many clients would say to me, "I see so much money coming in...where is it going...please help me save my business."

Geno going from a bank employee to being featured in magazines all across the country sounds like a dream come true for many of us. Of course, it wasn't always that easy for Geno. Sure, his joyful and genuine personality took him very far. But he's very well aware that there were many challenges along the way. Some that might have held him back at points, but mostly challenges that taught him powerful lessons that he can share with those he educates. When you take a look at your life right now, you're probably thinking about the current challenges you're facing. Most of us are constantly dealing with obstacles and setbacks, and some of us are facing the biggest ones we have ever had to face. But you know what? What you thought your biggest challenge was yesterday was followed by what you think your biggest challenge is today. And yes, tomorrow's challenge will feel even bigger than what you are facing right now. That is not to make you feel dread or despair. It is to make you aware of the realities of constantly stepping outside your comfort zone, one of the most rewarding habits you could ever pick up. Something that Geno told me that stuck out about challenges was that there is really only one challenge we all face that is consistent throughout our entire lives: YOU. Yes, you are your biggest challenge. Building self-discipline, self-worth, and constantly being around the right people is one challenge you should worry the most about. You really have to get yourself to the point of believing: "I can do this."

Geno says that surrounding himself with good company allowed him to be the best version of himself. "Great people around you bring out the greatness inside of you." Being around people who honor and respect you will really put you in a position to receive honest feedback that helps direct your growth in the right direction. It can be really easy to mistake bad advice for good advice when you are around the wrong people. Someone Geno considered to be a good friend told him that he needs to stop reaching out to younger people because he simply doesn't have the relatability anymore. Trusting this friend, Geno was thrown off and actually started to believe this. So he stopped doing it for a while. Until he realized it was terrible advice. But without that bad advice, Geno would never have directed that much more energy into working with the younger generation.

According to Geno, the beauty industry is one of the least discriminating industries. We don't care if you are straight or gay (or both), what your ethnicity is, or any of that. We embrace everyone, and for that reason, this industry warrants to have young professionals with refreshing minds, with the willingness to offer a beautiful personality and good heart above all. As a newbie, you need to know that there is always a place for you. It might not be behind the chair or a massage therapist, but it could be a manager, consultant, or even an educator. There are just so many opportunities beyond the salon's four walls. Open your eyes and see that the beauty industry is huge. Geno acknowledges that he himself never had any talent. Today he is considered an industry expert and Business Guru. It's because he chose to focus on *leading with a memorable personality*.

Geno left us with a few parting thoughts. "There is a place for everyone. Don't let your lack of skills in one area limit or discourage you." During hardships it can be difficult to realize that there are greater things on the horizon. Geno says that if you let your failures discourage you, you are only wasting the day. "Never overlook the fact that this is your life and your life is flying by." He then referred to a quote from John Lennon, "life is what happens while you're busy making other plans." Every day Geno asks himself two questions. In the morning, he asks himself, "How can I enhance my life and career and make them more rewarding?" This helps Geno *seek out the excitement in life*. "I don't wait for my life to unfold; I unfold it." Take time to sit with your thoughts and figure out how you can enhance your life and career to get the most out of your time here. The second question Geno asks himself right before bed is, "What don't I know that, if I did know, would make a difference in what I'm trying to become?" He goes on to say that this question helps him *fill the gap between where he is and where he could be*. "Everybody wants to be rich, but no one wants to fill the gap first." Figuring out what steps you need to take to become successful will create a foundation for you to build on.

CHAPTER 4:

PROTECT YOUR POCKETS

Amy Carter

N ow, personality is a big deal-breaker in the beauty industry. No matter how talented you are, likeability and passion are going to essentially be the WHY behind you standing out. Amy Carter, the owner of one of Indiana's top salons and founder of *Empowering You Consulting*, is a striking example of a woman whose passion to help others in the beauty industry took her from being thousands of dollars in debt, to running a multi-million dollar business. Amy, quite literally, started from the bottom. Her first exposure to the beauty industry was working at the front desk of a salon while attending college. She graduated with a degree in accounting, but she knew she wanted to be a small business owner. She knew at a young age that she had a passion for running small businesses.

It was here that she took the first life-defining step to buy a business. She got in touch with a potential partner, who happened to also be her babysitter and the person she worked for in college. After thorough research into the financial background of the business, she decided to take the step and buy into the business. She bought the business in a different state in October, while still enrolled in college, and moved there by late December. Mind you, the only reason she purchased a business was because of her newly-found love for small businesses and the beauty industry. Little did she know that her excitement and ambition to take-action would be the reason she ended up in debt so early on in her career. Shortly after arriving, she was met with confusion from existing employees that were already working there. Her partner had not informed anyone that there was a new partner joining the team, and so naturally, they assumed she was there for the front-desk opening. That should have been the first red flag. However, Amy was up for the challenge. Brushing it aside, Amy put in all of her energy into understanding the business' in-and-outs and essentially learning the basics of running a business. The deeper Amy got in, the more the truth about her partner began to surface. It turned out that Amy had just purchased a bankrupt business with a lot of debt attached to it. Her partner had hidden her buisness account and lied to lure Amy into purchasing her share, only to find out that they were several months behind in rent. Just like that, Amy found herself in a position where she was thousands of dollars in debt. Graduating from college, making a huge decision to buy into a business, and finding out you're broke and in debt is a horrible way to start out. She was making more money in college as a cocktail waitress than being a salon and spa owner.

If owning a business doesn't sound scary enough, Amy's story might just convince you *not* to rush into running your own business. It might have been the worst financial decision that Amy had ever made, despite having an accountant, a CPA (Certified Public Accountant), and even an attorney who helped her with the decision to purchase the business. However, she emphasizes how this experience actually helped her figure out what she wanted and what she didn't want in her next business. When her business partner skipped town in the middle of the night, and took all of her money, Amy had to figure out how to get herself out of debt, and quickly. The first thing she did was hire Susie Carder's company to help her figure out how to have more money coming in than going out, and was finally able to pay off all of her debt. Now, you don't have to follow Amy's footsteps and aim big so early on. But the big takeaway from this experience was the importance of maintaining a consistent flow of income in the process of building up your own business. One of the biggest tips Amy shared that helped her get out of debt was: get a job. Yes, a regular job that isn't exactly where you want to be in the next couple of years, but enough to help you sustain yourself so you don't have to live paycheck to paycheck. Often, when we think about the starting-from-scratch entrepreneur, we romanticize the struggle that comes with it. A little-known piece of advice is that you *should* keep your job because it is what is helping you pay the bills while allowing you to comfortably focus on your business strategies. One of the biggest mistakes you can make is rushing the process of building a business and essentially putting your pockets at risk. In fact, lack of preparation is exactly why so many salons and spa owners are living paycheck to paycheck.

Salon owners often first begin working as an employee at a salon or spa, and usually are under the misconception that the salon owner is probably making tons of money. So they think to themselves, *I could make a lot more money running my own salon.* This is true if you have the right strategy and help on your side. So they go ahead and rent a space, buy the equipment and products, and decide that their experience will get them as far as they need to go. But then, they are faced with bills they never even thought about. Insurance bills start piling up, fire extinguishers are maintained, and so on. What sounded simple in the first place becomes clearly too much for people to handle. The next thing that happens in such a scenario is that most of the money coming in ends up going to keep the salon running. The way I see it, the top two causes of poor financial management are: not having a plan and not knowing your numbers. It is easy to get caught up in work and everyday life, although it is crucial to have a financial plan in place. Something that you constantly have in your mind to make sure you are staying on track. Knowing your numbers comes down to how you track them and there are numerous ways to do this, such as purchasing a budget system or simply writing them in an Excel sheet.

Amy did her research and got help from an accountant, but still fell into a very commonly-faced trap that she didn't expect at all. So even with the right help and strategies, you're still very much at risk, and for that reason, you need to make sure that you know how to protect your pockets from the start. Amy took this bad experience and realized that it was time for her to figure out her financial situation before taking any more big steps. Her salon has hit over 1 million dollars a year for ten consecutive years, and she was able to move nine hours away from her business. She no longer considers herself as having a job, but as a successful business owner. With the right financial skill set, she was able to turn her losses into bigger wins. Like most of us who have made bad financial decisions, Amy wanted to give up. In 2008, the bank turned her revolving credit into a loan. Therefore, she had to start paying it back quickly, all in the midst of many employees walking out. Buying a bankrupt business had pushed Amy towards building financial skills, but the 2008 financial crisis is really the point at which Amy decided that enough was enough. It was time for financial freedom. This meant getting the help she needed and learning from the experts. When I asked Amy if there was anything she would change if she could do it all over again, she paused for a moment before smiling at me.

"Even on the darkest night, I would never change anything because if none of the bad things had happened, I wouldn't have reached where I am today."

Of course, we aren't saying that you should throw yourself into situations that put your pockets at risk. Rather, pick and choose what advice you take *very carefully*. The first step in protecting your pockets is to identify the subtle signs that you are having money problems. If you don't know what the signs are, you might not even realize that you DO have money problems. One of the signs is that your money is always on your mind and you have no idea where your money is even going. You are making minimum payments on high-interest debts, and you don't have a plan in place. Another sign is that you don't know, or aren't aware, of what your numbers are. Finally, hope is a large part of your financial strategy. Unfortunately, hope is NOT a strategy when it comes to money. Owners would sometimes encounter a crisis before they realize, "Shit, I could possibly lose everything!" You should know where every cent is going. As an owner, you should know what your retail budget and back bar budget are. What is your credit card percentage? You should know these answers off the top of your head. My biggest piece of advice that will save you thousands, and maybe even save your business, is to get a bookkeeper and/or CPA and a coach to better understand your finances to help you make smarter business decisions. Paying for these costs upfront will ensure you a prosperous business.

Once you have identified what your money problems are, the next step is to build your money management skills. The first principle to money is to spend less than what you earn; have more income than expenses. Seems so simple, yet so many business owners don't follow this principle. The second principle is to always plan for the future. The third principle is to help your money grow. Again, it sounds so easy, but for the beauty industry, it is not. The beauty industry is the second-highest industry to fail because of poor money management. If you don't have an accounting or finance degree like myself, you will need to hire a bookkeeper or, if not both, an accountant. Yes, we keep emphasizing the importance of hiring where you need help because too often business owners think they got it all under control until it is too late. From my experience, I would break down money management advice into the five following tips. The following are the minimum money management tips you should follow; there are plenty more out there.

1. Create a monthly budget and compare it to actual numbers
2. Track all of your expenses - no matter how small
3. Build a savings account, even if it takes time - because it will!
4. Pay your bills on time every month, or even pay them ahead of time
5. Review and cut back on recurring and unnecessary charges

Let's take a look at your own money management by completing the assessment below. From 1 to 10 (with 1 being the worst and 10 being the best) Be sure to answer these questions honestly. Add up your score so you have a starting point. Circle two or three things you would like to work on.

1. **I track my income monthly**
2. **I track my expenses monthly**
3. **I track all my expenses big or small**
4. **I have a money budget**
5. **I analyze budget numbers to actual numbers**
6. **I have a savings account with enough money to keep the business going for 3 months**
7. **Have a spreadsheet of all recurring expenses**
8. **Always pay bills on time**
9. **Pay interest on credit card monthly**
10. **Try to find new vendors with cheaper supplies**

Another way of protecting your pockets is making sure you price your services correctly. Now that you have money management in the works, it's time to consider whether you are pricing your services smartly. You should know the cost of each service and add up everything involved in the service. Take your total costs and multiply them by your desired profit margin percentage. Then add that amount to your costs. You have to know your fixed costs and variable costs to determine your break-even price. Never solely base your prices on competitor prices as they may not cover your costs. If your fixed costs are much higher than your competitors and your facials are the same price, you will be losing money on that service.

When protecting your pockets, you need to carefully consider when to decide to scale your business and hire more team members. For starters, you need a strong finance person, whether they be a bookkeeper or a CPA (Certified Public Accountant). This team provides financial information to allow you to attain goals and objectives in an organization. This person manages the preparation of balance sheets, profit and loss, and cash flow. The financial person helps in budgeting the business income. You need to plan where your money is spent, and how much is to be saved and invested. The finance person's objective is profit maximization. Again, your finances are the backbone of your business. Also, a strong management team, or person, is particularly significant if you want the business as a whole to grow and develop. Management becomes imperative for leadership responsibilities. The biggest part of your business is your technicians; they are the money producers. Remember, these are the people who you might spend more time with than your family. Make sure you like who they are, the type of person they are, and if they fit well in your company culture. It is worth noting that talent isn't everything when it comes to hiring technicians. Amy emphasizes that, when you hire, you need to look for a good human that loves what they do. It is possible to train everything else, but you don't want to waste too much time trying to fix your newbie's personality. How many people have been hired based on their talent, but ended up regretting it due to their personality? From financial support to front-desk services, make sure that everyone in the team fits your company's culture. When it comes to hiring, most people don't have any idea of what to look for and who to hire. It becomes one big "shit show." When it comes to hiring, the number one mistake that many people tend to make is hiring friends and family as their employees. Secondly, not giving clear expectations and direction ultimately sets the staff up to fail. Lastly, failure to listen to, help, and trust employees. Employees need to feel that their opinions matter and are valued. Employees absolutely need to be appreciated and valued; some people even find this more important than their paycheck!

A final tip to running a successful business and protecting your pockets is understanding the ins and outs of owning your space vs. renting. For this, let's break down the benefits and drawbacks of renting versus owning your own space.

Benefits of Owning Your Space or chair:

- Control over your schedule
- Design freedom: you have creative control over the look, feel, and culture
- You make the decisions
- You make the profit
- You learn management skills you potentially did not have prior

Drawbacks of Owning Your Space or chair:

- Administration work, and there is a lot of it
- Payment of taxes and insurances
- Losses if you are not managing the business successfully
- Everything is your responsibility: you know the saying "the buck stops here!"
- Dealing with employees
- Human Resources of employees
- Risk

Benefits of Renting Your Space:

- Set your own hours and schedules
- Make more money

- You decide your color or skincare lines
- Clients only deal with you
- Only paying a weekly/monthly fee for the chair or room

Drawbacks of Renting Your Space:

- A renter is responsible for growing their own clientele: many people struggle to do this on their own
- Schedule their own appointments: can become overwhelming
- Accounting and record-keeping
- Purchasing own supplies
- No benefits: such as paid time off and vacation time
- Pay your own taxes and insurance
- If you don't work, you still have to pay rent!

Looking back at Amy, she has mastered her financial freedom by growing her business and empowering her team to ensure the business is financially successful. As she moves the carrot forward to the next big thing, she is beginning to acknowledge that she has reached the point where she wants her employees to someday buy into the company. Her team has grown so strong that she sees that their loyalty and skills are of most value. The importance of teamwork will be covered in a later chapter, but for now, sit back and reflect on your own skill set. Where are your weaknesses and what are the steps YOU need to take to protect your pockets?

I, Karen, wanted to share this story with you. After you read it, please do not say it would never happen to you. It could happen to anyone so protect yourself.

I employed a Salon/Spa manager, Chris, and a hair manager, Steph, who were with me for 7 years. During the pandemic, while we were shut down, unbeknownst to me and everyone else, Chris and Steph decided to open their own hair salon down the road. When New York was allowing hair stylists to go back to work, they returned. A few weeks later, they left their resignation letters on my desk after we closed one night. Both letters stated they were ending their employment because a client came in with covid. Their new salon opened up the next day.

Both of these employees had keys to the building and complete access to our Spa Management System. They had contacted all of Luxe's hair clients, whether they saw them before or not. These employees started with me 7 years prior, without any clientele. I had spent thousands of dollars for their education, and they tried leaving with all clients they gained at Luxe. The worst part was watching the cameras and seeing them take hair supplies out the back door and high fiving each other in the parking lot. I will never forget seeing that.

CHAPTER 5:

CULTURAL CURRENCY

Damone Roberts

"**Y**ou. Here."

Damone Roberts looked up at Madonna, who had snapped her fingers and pointed to the space next to her. He frowned. *She did NOT just talk to me like that. Surely she wasn't talking to ME that disrespectfully.* Damone heard someone from her security team cough uncomfortably as Madonna looked at him straight in the eye.

"Oh no, honey," Damone responded assertively. "You have to say 'please'. We don't talk to people that way."

The reaction of the rest of the security team was very shocking, as Damone put it, they were 'clutching their pearls'. This was THE Madonna, as in Madonna Louise Ciccone who also happened to be one of Damone's biggest idols. Yet, here he was telling her off for disrespecting him. You see, Damone is a fine example of someone who believes in himself and in his talent so strongly that he knows his worth, where to stand up for himself and for what he believes in. In this case, it was his belief that it is your birthright to be respected. This confidence allowed him to reach unimaginable heights. Today, Damone Roberts' name is synonymous with creating iconic beauty and for his renowned talent of sculpting the perfect arch. He is known for painting the features and shaping the brows of some of the world's prominent beauties and famous faces, including Madonna, Oprah, Beyoncé, Rihanna, Kim Kardashian, Ariana Grande, Taraji P. Henson, Channing Tatum, Alicia Keys, Christina Aguilera, Nicki Minaj, Robert Downey Jr. and many more.

So how did Damone get from hanging up Madonna posters in his bedroom to telling her off on the first day of meeting her in person? Damone acknowledges that, quite frankly, he was always naturally gifted with his hands as an artist. He traces his success back to a fateful day in high school when he decided to take part in a worldwide contest to win a scholarship at Rutgers University. At the time, it was a very *"ah, why the hell not?"* move. So he quickly put together a sketch of Diana Ross, for which he won first place in the contest. Oh, and by the way, fast forward a couple of years later, not only did Damone get to actually meet Diana Ross, but she also expressed to him that she loves using his products.

Winning this contest meant that Damone was able to go to Rutgers University on a scholarship, an experience that he credits to his early discovery for his passion for the beauty industry. Being around other artists made him feel for the first time that he belonged somewhere. Damone had grown up feeling really out of place, mainly because he didn't fit in with any other group in high school. A key lesson he learned from his Rutgers education is the importance of emphasizing certain features and deemphasizing other features, and essentially the importance of balance and structure. He thought wow, this applies to eyebrows, but also to life itself. His college experience is also what allowed him to commit to always being true to himself, even if it meant weirding people out. That attribute paid off, and as we have discussed in previous chapters, contributed heavily to having a memorable personality.

In one of his college make-up classes, he had a teacher explain to him that make-up design is essentially just painting a person's face instead of a canvas. That was the lightbulb moment where everything clicked. *There's something to this.* The fact that you could use make-up to help someone achieve a look that they envisioned, whether it be by making their nose smaller or lips bigger, gave him the inspiration he needed. His next step was getting a job at a make-up counter at the mall. He had initially been working at Costco, making the most amount of money that he had ever made at that time, but he was miserable. Damone made a promise to himself that no matter how good the pay was, he would never allow himself to do something he didn't love. It was there that he sent out his application to MAC Cosmetics. Back in the '90s, MAC was the *"IT"* move, as it was the biggest cosmetics brand at the time. It was where all of the cool people shopped, worked, and were!

After sending in the three different application parts, which constituted a day look, a night look, and a random selection look, Damone got accepted to work with MAC. A common mistake many people in the beauty industry make is thinking that they have learned all they need to learn. Looking back at my conversation with Anika, this was something that both Anika and Damone would agree on. No matter how far along you've gone, you're always going to be learning more. This might sound like a very simple lesson, but in reality, it is the underlying attitude that every successful feature in this book has. With Damone, even today he is still learning more techniques with eyebrows; from how brows can lift the cheekbones to how they can bring out chin definition. Another thing that Damone shares in common with the others in this book is his *passion*. He always went after what he loved, knowing that money would eventually follow through afterward.

His reasons for leaving a relatively high-paying position at Costco to working at a low-paying position in MAC were very simple. He loved the culture, and he loved being able to show up to work in whatever clothes he felt expressed his personality, so long as it met the Mac black branding. Yes, that meant that on some days he would show up with an all-black outfit and matching black rollerblades. After working in Mac, his talent, passion, and drive propelled him to be called to do performance artists. Before long, he was doing eyebrows for the *90210* sets and, quite quickly, building a name for himself in the beauty industry. His instinctive move to start working at Mac instead of listening to his parents who advised him to find a more serious and sustainable career paid off. Fast forward a couple of more years, Damone ended up being the face of Mac for eyebrows and even helped them design their own eyebrow product line.

Damone has done it all. There are a lot of defining moments in his career that made him realize, *I have finally made it*. Sure, we could say it was the moment he was able to tell Madonna to be nice or he's out, or even the day he met the very same celebrity that he drew for his college scholarship competition. But when I asked him, he paused for a moment before telling me about his feature in the T.V. show *Jeopardy*. Damone was driving home one day and got a call from his friend telling him that some blonde-haired kid won a couple of thousand dollars for guessing his name as the right answer. It didn't end there. Again, he got a call from another friend who told him that while playing the *Trivial Pursuit* board game, they stumbled on a question asking: "What parts of madonna have been plucked by Damone Roberts?" Damone, quite literally, went from putting up wall posters of his idols to being featured in board games and T.V. shows for working with them.

His inspiration lies, not in a singular person, but rather in all of his clients. He describes the process of eyebrow-plucking as something similar to a therapy session. Having the client laying back with their head practically in his lap while he works his art, whether it is Oprah Winfrey or the young girl who saved up for months for the chance to get her eyebrows done by Damone Roberts, is a very intimate moment. Much like a sponge, Damone very easily absorbs all the life lessons that he can from his clients. Connecting with them is an essential part of his learning experience, one that he values very dearly. When he shared this with me, it really got me thinking of the importance of building your ideal clientele. At the end of the day, those who come to you are definitive of your image, regardless of what position and specific part of the industry you work in.

An ideal client is someone who finds the perfect solution to their problems/needs in the services/products your company provides. Your ideal client will be loyal to you, will frequently buy your services/products, and will recommend your company to friends. When you don't know who to market to, you end up marketing to everybody and that is a sure recipe for failure! Determining your ideal client will make it apparent who is not your ideal client. Every technician goes through it; you look at your schedule for the day and see a name that you are just not excited for, someone who just drains all your energy. That person is not your ideal client! An easy place to start looking and determining who your ideal client would be is your existing clientele! You know them and what they are looking for, so check in to see if they are the clients who you are looking for. Get down to the nitty-gritty and write down specifics of your ideal client, such as age bracket, what industry they work in, location, and income level. Think about where and what they do in their free time, and what hobbies do they like; try to come up with 20 characteristics! All of these things are important to know about your ideal client as you need to know how to market to them!

Once you have defined who your ideal client is, you need to then take the steps to attract this person. There are systems that need to be put in place in order to effectively get this done. For starters, determine what makes your salon and spa unique and run with it! In order to attract your ideal client, you should know how they make their purchasing decisions - some people purchase impulsively; some take time to research and read reviews. Knowing how your ideal client purchases goods and services such as yours will be beneficial when it comes to marketing and sales! Once you have figured out how to attract the ideal client, the next step is working on increasing your clientele. First and foremost, social media should be your best friend. Putting yourself and your brand/company on social media platforms allows for everyone to see - and not just the people who follow you. Implement social media strategies! Running promotions will also help increase your clientele - you could start small and work your way up to larger promotions that will attract more people. Ratings and reviews - feedback to you and your brand should be extremely important to you! If someone sees a bad review, it will alter their decision on your establishment. So, be sure to keep an eye on your reviews and don't be afraid to share reviews on your social media channels.

If I could break it down for you, there are a couple of major tips to consider. One is leveraging your already-existing clientele. Ask for referrals from all your clients, friends, and family! Ask clients who love you to write a review. Reviews should not be a simple, "Kevin is great," but rather along the lines of, "Kevin transformed my look with highlights that gave me the gorgeous dimension and a precision cut!" Your network is your net worth, and this applies here too. Always, ALWAYS network! For example, after working all day you get a bite to eat at a restaurant, and the waitress asks, "how are you tonight?" Your response is "I'm so exhausted because I had so many clients today." This is a great way to open the networking conversation and the waitress' curiosity is piqued, and BOOM. Brand new client, and dinner! Don't forget to carry business cards with you! New clients aren't the only way to grow your clientele; keep that in mind too. You also need to keep reaching out to old or missing clients. Continue to do these things every day, because when you stop marketing yourself you will not notice right away. But rest assured that three months down the road when your number of clients per day declines, you'll definitely notice!

Now that you have built a solid lead flow, you need to make sure you have a good system for customer retention. Think: what should you do to keep your clients coming back? *What's in it for them*? One of the biggest things that I implement at my salon is a loyalty program! For every dollar spent they receive points. Once they get 2000 points, they get a $50 gift card towards any product or service. Another reason why clients continue to come back is plain old customer service - whether it be a client's first or 100th time in, we will always treat them the same way! It is imperative for clients to know and feel like we value them! A simple rule that makes a difference - my staff tries to get to know new clients even if they are not their current provider. Clients love when everyone pays attention to them and allows them to feel welcomed! Learning and remembering little details such as how the client takes their coffee, will make a world of difference as well! Treat every client like they are the only client you are seeing all day long!

As Damone put it, our main purpose in the beauty industry is that *we bring out the best version of people.* His personal brand centers around this mission to provide high-end brow services to virtually anyone by making them accessible. He shared with me a very special memory of his when he saw a young woman from the projects come all the way to his salon in Manhattan and sit down next to another client that has had multiple magazine features. This client is one of the world's richest women, according to Forbes. Now, these two clients didn't really know the others' story, but Damone did. As he watched them scroll through their phones as they waited for their turn, he realized that these two clients may have two completely different lives, but here they are sitting right next to each other because of a shared purpose: to bring out the best versions of themselves through beauty. They came in with their shoulders low, and because of his magic, they left the salon with their shoulders up and their hair flying in the breeze. This is what we do.

Instead of an assessment, this chapter has a worksheet for you to fill out to help you determine your ideal client.

- **Age**

- Gender
- Location
- Income
- Occupation
- Personality
- Values
- Opinions
- Attitudes
- Types of lifestyle
- Interests
    - Social media interests
    - Reading interests

Think about WHO you want to walk into the doors of your salon/ spa as you fill out the above worksheet. The more concise you are, the more you can market to clients you want.

CHAPTER 6:

TEAMWORK MAKES THE DREAM WORK

Kelly Smith

Kelly grew up heavily involved in dance and gymnastics. Her first job was teaching at a dance studio at 14 years old. From this young age, Kelly knew that she wanted to be in an environment where women supported one another. She also knew that she wanted to start her own business in order to be the boss.

Kelly has a degree in sociology from the University of Washington. She is really fascinated by how to make groups work together. After her college graduation, she started working for a general contractor in Bellevue, WA as a backup receptionist. She quickly worked her way up to contract management and marketing. Eventually, she ran their marketing department and then reached the board/committee level at the company. This was a family-owned business and the owners basically adopted Kelly into their family. They let her do whatever she wanted in terms of which department she was involved in. This freedom allowed Kelly to experience different aspects of the business and determine what she liked and disliked. When the general contracting company hired a management consultant, she was their right-hand woman. Kelly helped create systems to forecast income, manage relational databases, and determine who was working on what. Eventually, Kelly was offered ownership in the company. When this opportunity came knocking at her door, she had to decide whether or not she wanted to work in a male-dominated industry. She realized she didn't want to wear steel-toe boots, walk in the mud, or mess her hair up with a hard hat; and she also felt like she wouldn't be taken seriously in this male dominated industry. She didn't know the industry inside out; she only knew the business side and didn't want to be part owner of something that she didn't fully understand.

Kelly realized she was really passionate about systems and scaling. Scaling a business means adding revenue at a faster rate than they tack on new costs. These things came naturally to her; it was easy for her to see what a business needed in order to grow and flourish. At this point in her life, she was teaching aerobics instead of dance. Something she would look forward to was her facial every few weeks. Kelly described this pampering as her "guilty pleasure." She loved the softer side of the business she found in the beauty industry. She decided she would pursue her dreams by opening a day spa. In 1999, Kelly opened her own day spa and made seven figures within a couple of years, which less than 1% of spas do. Her sister helped her run the business but was only in town half of the time so she could spend time with her family. The other half of the time, Kelly had to do everything herself. After Kelly had her second child, she realized that she needed to make some changes in order to spend more time with her family. *"I was raising a husband and two children and 20 employees."* She decided to sell the business. Kelly reached out to her competitors and the first person she spoke to bought the spa. After selling her business, she said to herself "I'll never own a small business again; it's too hard." Soon after the sale of her spa, she started doing business consulting for restaurant owners, and earned her real estate license. She did a little bit of real estate agent work in addition to consultant work for different businesses.

One day, Kelly saw her friend for botox. She mentioned two doctors who really needed Kelly's help. The surgeons operated a medical spa in Coeur D'Alene, Idaho. Kelly met with the two doctors and they told her they wanted normal working hours, and to not be on call. At this point the doctors were only doing laser and vein services. Kelly told them straight out there's no way of that happening with these services. They needed to be doing 5-10 thousand dollar surgeries. The doctors were also spending $20,000 on image advertising with no call-to-action; which was resulting in no business growth. Kelly knew immediately they needed a higher ticket price to find clients. After researching, she discovered Smart Lipo by Cynosure. The doctors agreed to buy this machine and went for training. While the doctors were at training, Kelly sold the Smart Lipo Procedure to ten clients. They were shocked Kelly generated interest in this new service. They did $1 million in the first 10 months. Kelly was able to increase the company's revenue from $800,000 to $4 million in two years. She understood where the doctors' problems stemmed from, and turned this business into a profitable one. Kelly increased their exposure by speaking at conferences around the country.

This began Kelly's successful consulting business. She discovered that scaling a company had a lot to do with building a positive company culture. One of her biggest challenges was taking a million-dollar company to a multi-million-dollar company. Kelly realized top management are usually the people who didn't want to change. Top management has to learn how to delegate the right way and motivate people to build on their behalf. This is imperative because employees won't value you until you value them.

The ego is a powerful thing. Ego is part of the self that gets a business off the ground. However, it is not the thing that helps a business grow. A leadership mindset is different from the business mindset it takes to grow a business. Company leaders need to put their egos aside and realize that they are not always going to be the best; but they should treat their employees with

RAGS TO RICHES

respect and motivate them to help scale the business. A company's culture must include trust for both the employees and managers to make decisions in the best interest of the company. When this happens, day-to-day operations run smoothly. Clear operating instructions in a company must be carried out to hold people accountable in a way that is fair to everyone. *"The icing on the cake is when you finally get to the top part of the company."* It is important for company leaders to look at themselves in the mirror and realize problems might stem from them. "People do what you do, not what you say. If you don't like the company culture, then you have to take a look at yourself."

A defining moment in Kelly's career was when she wrote her first book. Her book, <u>Top 10 Profit Killers for Plastic Surgeons and Medical Spas,</u> includes things that she does with her clients every day. It was helpful for her clients and even other business owners to read this book to get a taste of what she does in her consulting business. Kelly believes every business problem comes down to two things: company culture and the person at the top.

As a business consultant, her main job is working with people and making sure they can collaborate in a productive way to grow and sustain a business. Throughout her career, she has seen a lot of success stories. Kelly's inspiration is watching people grow and do things they weren't able to do before; like take a vacation or switch to a four day work week and still make a profit. Kelly enjoys watching her female employees succeed and do a job that they take pride in. Kelly knows the benefit of making sure every one of her employees feels valued. It is important that employees know she appreciates them and all of their hard work. A few things that Kelly does are: send her staff monthly gifts and host a yearly gathering.

"The most expensive advice is bad advice from someone who isn't qualified." Kelly spent $15,000 to join Darren Hardy's high-performance forum. Even though this is a huge amount of money, she wanted to continue her education. Kelly got advice from many people on how to deal with a toxic director she hired. She was nervous to terminate this person due to the fact the director wore many hats and did good work. However, she was very toxic and it affected the rest of her employees. During the forum, she realized as a leader, it was her job to create a positive work environment. Darren told her there was no way for her to take the entitlement out of an employee, and assured her that everything would work out for the best. After the decision to let the director go, her team rallied around her with love and support. "This was when I fell in love with my company. I had to do a trust fall and hope they would catch me."

These two quotes really stuck with Kelly. *"Just keep swimming,"* from the Disney movie Finding Nemo, inspires her even when the water's current is pushing back. Another quote is from Wayne Gretsky, *"You miss 100% of the shots you don't take."* She applies this quote to other areas of her life such as business, taking risks, learning new things, and putting herself out there. She feels these are keys to growing and becoming a more educated professional.

"Learning new things is the secret to happiness."

A business leader's job is much more than providing a space to earn a paycheck. Providing a safe environment will bring out employees' creativity, talent, and passion for their work. It's as simple as that.

It is important to consider that there are many people who don't feel like they belong at home. Providing a sense of belonging generates excitement just from the environment. It's imperative to design a safe, loving environment that brings out the stylist's passion and creativity.

The future of your business is 99% based on who is a part of your team. You need to attract the best of the best.

I believe one thing you need to do is set standards. But how do you go about determining what these standards are? A code of conduct is the most common policy within an organization. It portrays the company's principles, standards, and the moral and ethical expectations that employees are held to. Your code of conduct should clarify your company's mission, values, and principles. Having a dedicated code of conduct will enhance your company's core values, beliefs, and set the tone for your company's culture. It will also build your reputation and give a vision and mission to the company.

There are different types of codes of conduct. Some examples are: dress code, employee behaviors, tardiness/absenteeism, leave/vacation policy, employee break policy, conflicts of interest, and communication. Your code of conduct should include elements such as integrity, teamwork, respect, innovation, and client focus. Determine your company culture, and evaluate how you think your business should be running.

Codes of conduct should always be adjusted and updated. An extensive employee handbook should contain all codes of conduct, along with other information that employees will need to know. With new hires, we sit down and go through the handbook together so they have a deep understanding of the company's policies. It is a contract between the employer, Luxe Salon Spa and Laser Center, and employees. This is why I always have myself and the new hire sign the handbook. This will be part of the employee's file. Be sure to give them a copy of the signed document.

I believe systems are vital to operate and grow a high functioning business. Everything that happens on a consistent basis should have a set procedure. For example, you will always need to order more products. Therefore, you should have an ordering system in place. Structuring these systems leads to more efficiency, and it will allow you to operate at a higher level which will ultimately increase profits.

Creating new systems and procedures can be hard. A great way to start is by looking at what is simply not working, or isn't working how you had hoped. You need to think about everything, such as the steps you're taking, the tools you're using, how much time the process takes, the cost, and the types of results you're getting.

Sit down with your answers and plan your new process. Make a list of systems you want to change. Start by prioritizing which system is most important and determine the essential steps and most efficient sequence. Check to see if there is a machine or software system that can be implemented to aid in the systems improvement.

I know my team has to be part of this process, and they must buy into it in order for it to be successful. Each year at our annual meeting, we review the mission, vision, and principles as a team, then we give it our blessing or change it if needed. I don't simply make things up with what I want and pray the team buys into it — it doesn't work that way. Your mission/vision should not only be in line with your (the owner's) thoughts but also of your employees. Valuing your employees' feedback and opinions should be of great importance to you, and that is what makes them "buy into" our vision.

When employees feel heard, they are more inclined to harness their creativity and demonstrate their passion. Again, it is a joint effort between employees and owners to come up with incentive programs. This is because these incentives are what will motivate employees the most to work hard to meet their goals! For instance, if they hit their quarterly goal, then they will get a determined amount of money, depending on how much they exceeded it! My team loves money. I mean, who doesn't?

Hiring the right people and keeping them for the long haul is crucial to building a successful business! Turnover costs U.S. companies one trillion a year — yes, with a T! Not a million or billion, but one trillion dollars! Replacing an employee can cost anywhere from one-half to two times the said employee's annual salary. Employee retention leads to better customer experiences, more consistency and momentum across the company, and strong company culture! When turnover is low and engagement is high, companies can more easily attract the right people for the job.

The top things to keep in mind are hiring the right people, optimizing the onboarding experience with new hires, creating a culture of recognition and feedback, developing your employees' careers, and asking questions in exit surveys. After being in the industry for over 30 years, it is essential to **hire slow and fire fast**. You will know in your gut when an employee will just not work out, so don't hold on to them hoping that something will change. Nothing will change. When I first started out as an owner, I would hire anyone with a heartbeat! I had to learn to develop patience for interviews and navigate the right candidates for the job.

Another idea for your team is being partners with other companies. Employees are the core of your team, but even those that you partner up with add to the culture of your business. Creating partnerships with outside companies can be a great idea, although they need to be mutually beneficial to all parties involved. Partnerships are important to build your brand and your audience. Partnerships can raise more awareness for your brand, meaning more sales.

For instance, my salon/spa partnered with a high-end country club in the surrounding area to allow members our services at a small discounted rate. We also offered special deals to the club members that were not offered to normal clients around the holidays! Another partnership we have is with a local athletic club; their members get discounts on our services and we hand out their promotional flyers with our gift card sales. Picking and choosing outside partnerships should be considered carefully. Your mission, vision, and core values must be aligned!

At this point, you're probably a little overwhelmed by all of this information. For that reason, you might want to re-read each chapter and make notes when necessary. I have one final tip to give: find the balance between your work and personal life. This is relevant to building your team because, at the end of the day, the way you carry yourself both in and out of the office speaks volumes to your employees.

My motto is to work hard and play hard! Work-life balance means something different to everyone; just because these tips work for me, doesn't necessarily mean they will work for you. A trick that works for me is "unplugging." Nowadays, technology makes us available around the clock — it is important to me to be off my phone and spend quality time with family. My husband, Jim, and I have two daughters, and the saying "time flies" is so true when it comes to raising our kids. My family time is precious to me.

Other than that, my top tips for having a good work-life balance are to prioritize your time, have personal time, set work hours and stick to them, make your workspace for you, and don't spread yourself too thin. I have always loved to work out as I have made it part of my routine since high school. I spend the first hour of every day working out and that makes me feel human. You will need to think about what is important in your life and value the time you need to take in order to enjoy it. The grind is real, but so is the self-care. Start small and build from there. Remember, committing to drastic changes is a recipe for failure. You know, it's like starting a strict diet... it never works. Take time to come up with and figure out what type of work-life balance works for you.

Many times, you will get a candidate through the interview process. You have offered the job, and they have accepted. Many salon and spa owners will have the employees start immediately, with no onboarding process.

In this chapter, I will provide you with my onboarding checklist for employees instead of an assessment:

- **Federal State and government paperwork**
- **Company handbook**
- **Dress code**
- **Business cards, smock, name tag**
- **Company directory**

- **Payroll schedule**
- **Sexual Harassment Policy**
- **Company meetings schedule**
- **Day off/Vacation request forms**
- **Punch in/out/break**

Before even getting started with orientation, training, and settling in, you need to make sure that the above checklist is complete and your employee is officially ready to join the team!

CHAPTER 7:

REVERSE PLANNING -
DESTINY IS CALLING

Matthew Collins

"If your son decides to get into cutting hair and all that stuff, just make sure that he gets into education. That's where all the money is."

Crazy as it might sound, these words were spoken by a beauty equipment supplier to Matthew Collins' father way back when he was a kid. His dad had gone to get him a set of clippers because Matthew had been begging him to take him to get his hair cut every week. Little did this random guy know that Matthew would one day be the Global Styling Ambassador for Dyson and signed to the world's most well-known celebrity artist agency. Matthew's work, advice, and tips have been featured in many online and print publications such as Vogue, GQ, People, Elle Canada, Elle Serbia, FASHION, Flare, The Kit, The Globe and Mail, InStyle, Ion, and Salon Magazines. Collins' celebrity clients have included Gigi Hadid, Paris Jackson, Kristen Stewart, Dua Lipa, Hailey Baldwin, Priyanka Chopra, Bryce Dallas Howard, Kristen Bell, Madison Beer, Hunter Schafer, Mandy Moore, Julia Fox, Emma Chamberlain, Lili Reinhart and Joe Keery. Matthew has also been the official Hair Expert on The Social, E! Network's Celebrity Style Story, and ETalk Canada.

Now, Matthew didn't even know that this random beauty supplier had unknowingly predicted his future, until much later when his dad shared the story with him. Between the age of 12 and 17, Matthew was so engrossed in the idea of cutting hair that he would cut his own hair every three days. At this point, he realized that all his friends were getting really terrible haircuts. That's when he decided that he would offer to help them out with their haircuts. With an air of confidence in his talent, he promised them a $50 guarantee if he messed their hair up. Of course, Matthew never ended up having to pay anyone $50. Although, he admits that at the time, he had no idea what he was doing, and was probably holding the scissors all wrong. He was able to get a basic idea of proportions. At no point did he ever want to be a professional hairdresser, but he just knew that he loved it. After failing to achieve success in university, he was determined to try again. He also ended a toxic relationship that had been leading nowhere. He began to ask himself some tough questions: *What am I really doing with my life? Which path should I be taking?* With no clear direction, he felt lost and confused.

Through all of this, Matthew was still cutting hair. He hadn't really experienced a salon, with his own experience being limited to the monthly trips to the barber. So the idea of entering the beauty industry just hadn't clicked yet. As the pressure and confusion began to pile up and became too much for him, Matthew broke down in the car with his mom. Gently, she brought to his attention the passion he had for cutting hair. Surely there was some potential there, right? It was what he loved. She encouraged him to try shadowing the hairdresser that she regularly went to. After all, what did he have to lose? Unsure what to expect, Matthew walked into the salon the next weekend with skater shoes, khaki shorts, and a golf shirt to start work by sweeping the floors. Now, Matthew prides himself on being a punctual person and his fiance always makes fun of him for setting up at least 5 to 10 backup alarms. However, on the second day of work, the alarms didn't go off and he was half an hour late to work.

Devastated, he pulled his boss aside and profusely apologized. It was then at that moment what he had internally desired all his life, came out. He explained that he was extremely grateful for this opportunity and his dream was to move to LA and become a celebrity hairdresser. It wasn't until this point that Matthew even realized what he really wanted to do. After all, working in the beauty industry isn't something that we are encouraged to consider from a young age. It's often a decision we make much later along the way as we begin to uncover our talent and passion. Matthew's story is one that begins with a young man who was confused about his purpose in life and where he is meant to be. If it wasn't for his mother pointing out the obvious love he had for cutting hair, he probably would've taken a lot longer to get where he is today. However, once he knew what he loved and what he was good at, moving forward it really just became about moving with purpose and being truly self-aware about what his next steps were. Not only do you need to act with intention, but you need to also take these next steps based on WHO you want to be. So how can we do this? How can we take what we envision ourselves to be and turn it into action steps? It all comes down to knowing what **needs to be done** and what **not** to do.

Once Matthew began to move in the direction of his dreams, he began to accumulate the experience and knowledge that got him to where he is today. Today, Collins is a Canadian-born hair stylist and colorist, based in LA with a career spanning more than 15 years. Collins is a Global Dyson brand ambassador. He travels across Canada, and internationally, teaching his craft. He's also worked regularly on the hair teams for Paris and Toronto Fashion Weeks. Something to note is that Matthew was always a very meticulous person. He knew *specifically* who his ideal clientele would be. We've already discussed ideal clients in previous chapters, but Matthew really shines in the clientele department. His written ideal client characteristics were over a page long, not just some bullet points that he thought of. For instance, he knew the exact age range, industry worked in, salary, female, attractive if they posted on social media at least four times a week. He was ahead of the game with choosing the right 'influencers' to work with! He knew that knowing who his ideal client is, was his key to success. Matthew, in general, put a lot of thought into who he wanted to be. He directed his focus 100% on what he was doing, who his clientele was, how much money he wanted to make, how many hours he would be working, etc. Every aspect of his plan was completely intentional of where he wanted to be!

He declared that he wanted to be a celebrity stylist, and started researching! He found top photographers, fashion designers, models, and stylists. He studied all of these people's work and choices to decide what path he wanted to take for himself. He was very methodical of where he wanted to be and what he wanted to accomplish. His next step was to write down his professional goals; one-year goals, five-year goals, ten-year goals, and the top three tasks that he would need to do in order to accomplish those goals. By being so systematic, he was able to accomplish his five-year goal in only three years - the goal of doing an international brand campaign for L'oreal.

Whenever I have someone come up to me with an unclear vision of where they want to direct their lives, even though they know for sure that it is somewhere in the beauty industry, I tell them to take a little assessment. Take out a piece of paper and try to be as detailed as possible. **Ask yourself the following questions.**

1. **Can you clearly define your ideal intention? What is your end goal?**
2. **Do you know your time frame?**
3. **What resources will you need in order to meet your goal?**

4. **Do you want a partner?**

5. **Do you want to own alone?**

6. **Do you have a marketing plan or have a silent partner?**

7. **Do you have a social media plan?**

8. **Do you have 1-year goals? 5-year goals? 10-year goals?**

9. **Do you have financial goals?**

Now, keep in mind that the assessment isn't a one-and-done thing! It is a work in progress, so you should review your goals weekly to make sure you are staying on track! From this assessment, you can extract the main action steps that need to be taken. The process is one that requires you to dig deeper, and so guidance is always needed to make sure you are digging in the right places. For this reason, I highly recommend that you check out the *Rags to Riches In Action* companion course as it will help you in turning the answers to these questions into tangible action steps. Are you ready to take action? To have the process work, and work effectively - it takes blood, sweat, and tears!

The question of who you want to be can be a difficult one. Yes, it is a heavy question, it's not the question you start with. Going through the process leads up to this final question and it is for that reason that you need to have a structured approach to conducting this assessment. One of Matthew's favorite quotes is, *"you must sacrifice who you are to become who you want to be."* The selection of questions you ask yourself can make or break your assessment process, and it is for this reason that you need to understand what successful people like Matthew went through, and what they learned. For example, at one point, he had a business partner that he opened a salon with and that business relationship ended acrimoniously. However, Matthew learned a great deal from that experience. The more you can write out a plan, breaking it down into smaller steps or action items, the more you will notice the difference - this should be a well-thought-out process. The good news is that this book, and our companion course, give you the exact resources you need to go from rags to riches.

When I first started, I only had a spa. About six months later, I acquired more space to open a salon. A great friend of mine was a hairstylist named Leah, and she came to Luxe to be the salon manager. It started out great and we were extremely successful! As the success at Luxe grew, Leah became disgruntled that I was the owner, despite her being paid generously. Our friendship started to deteriorate, and she started giving other employees a hard time and was being disrespectful. The situation escalated to the point of a physical fight breaking out between four employees. The two other employees involved had to seek refuge in my office and alerted me of the situation. I sent my husband to the spa because I knew if I were the one to go, it would be an even bigger disaster. My husband walked everyone to their cars and made sure they left for the evening. At that point, I called Leah and fired her. It was a hard decision to make, we were like sisters at one point, but she had become too resentful and jealous. The moral of the story is, do not work with family or friends, and make sure to have a detailed contract.

CHAPTER 8:

BRANDING AND EXPANDING

Julie Kandalec

"In my English paper, I actually wrote 'What I want to be when I grow up: model, actress, lawyer, or a manicurist.'"

Julie knew, from as young as 12, that she absolutely loved nails. She saw and appreciated the nail aspect of beauty for what it was; less of an accessory part of one's looks, and more a form of artistic and cultural expression. Some people have to spend some time trying out a lot of new things before finding their perfect fit in the beauty industry, much like Matthew in the previous chapter. For others, however, the dream of building a career in the beauty industry has always been found within and has given them the drive towards their goals as early as possible.

Julie's perseverance and eagerness from such a young age were channeled directly into building the skills and knowledge necessary to reach where she wanted to be. By the time she was 17, Julie had graduated from cosmetology school at the top of her class. That was just the beginning of her prosperous career! One thing that Julie was able to master that put her ahead of many others was to break down nail care further beyond just polish. She always felt in touch with her inner creative side, taking the time to simultaneously train in painting, drawing, color, and dance. This allowed her to see nail care in ways many others around her did not, because they hadn't fully submerged themselves into the art as Julie did. Alongside her strategic, yet instinctive, submersion into various different forms of artistic expression to polish her own main focus on nails, Julie also has a personalized touch that has left a mark on many. Known for her gentle touch, calm demeanor, and precise attention to detail, Julie's specialties vary from a clean, natural nail to elaborate, custom-designed nails. To cap this talent, Julie's work can now be seen in Allure, Vanity Fair, Cosmopolitan, Marie Claire, V, and Vogue.

So how does Julie's story bring us to branding and expanding? Good question. By the time Julie decided to announce her global nail academy in 2019, then called Masterclass Nail Academy, rebranded as Julie K Nail Academy in May 2022, she had branded herself magnificently in the nail beauty industry. However, she knew that now she had built a powerful brand image and wanted to expand. Her expertise allowed her to provide education to salons, spas, and hotel resorts on a *worldwide* scale. Not settling for any less than she dreams of, Julie went on to launch her first retail product, a 42-page creative workbook simply titled "Nail Art Design Book" the following year. In early 2021, amidst the pandemic, she celebrated the launch of her private nail atelier, Julie K Nail ARTelier in Manhattan's Financial District. Julie is a great example of how one can expand their skills as a brand and as a business owner by thinking outside the box. Today, that gives her the ability to comfortably do what she loves while being able to jump on a plane to travel wherever she wants to, whenever she wants to.

Before we continue further into Julie's story, let's take a little pause and look back at the concept of branding. We've all at least heard of how important branding is, or maybe even dissected what branding consists of. Branding is extremely important as it's how customers recognize and experience your business! Branding is your business' selling point; how you stand out against the rest. Branding consists of logos, taglines, and jingles, all the way to what fonts and colors are being used. For example, my salon and spa's colors are white, black, and red. When creating new marketing tools, our team sticks to the same colors so that way when someone thinks of Luxe Salon, Spa & Laser Center, those colors and our logo come to mind. We also have our tagline, 'isn't it time for some Luxe in your life?'. It is important to keep in mind that you are trying to make your brand stand out. What makes you different, what makes you unique, how do you stand out against the rest? I branded Luxe as an upscale salon, spa, and laser center with high-end services and products. I knew that I wanted its personality to be friendly, clean, and sophisticated! We always say we cater to the masses, not the asses!

Done correctly and strategically, branding will be the number one leverage you can use to expand and scale your business, simply based on the impression you leave on clients. Clients will always remember your brand from the way you present yourself. The visual representation of your brand will be their reference point; be sure to build that correctly, as the options to expand are endless. Building your brand comes down to the question: who is your target audience? The more specific your target audience, the more in-depth you can craft your brand's identity. In previous chapters, we talked about how to determine your ideal client. To refresh your memory, determining your ideal client starts with looking at your current clientele. What is their job, how old are they, how much money do they make, how far do they live? These are all questions you should be asking yourself in order to find your ideal client, and therefore build your brand! Your ideal clientele comes down to who you want to serve. You will know in your heart who is the right client for you, and certainly who is not.

So you've figured out who to tailor your brand identity too. Now what? The next step I would direct you to would be to tackle the five key brand elements:

1. **Brand Position** - this is the part of the brand that describes what you do and for who, what makes your brand unique, and how customers benefit from your brand.

2. **Brand Promise** - this is the most important thing that your brand promises to deliver to your customers. Consider what your customers, employees, and partners should expect from every interaction.

3. **Brand Personality** - this is where you illustrate what your brand wants to be known for. Think of personality traits you want to be tied to your brand. You should ideally have four to six traits.

4. **Brand Story** - your brand's story illustrates the history of the brand; this adds value and credibility to your brand.

5. **Brand Associations** - these are the specifics of your brand such as name, logo, color, fonts, taglines, imagery, etc. Your brand associations should all correlate to the brand's traits and support your statement.

Your brand really is just an avatar in itself. When you envision your brand, take a moment to really reflect on what this avatar would look like and how they would act. Characterize your brand to find its personality. Is it exciting? Is it sincere? Sophisticated? You should pick roughly three to five personality traits (or adjectives) that you want people to think of when thinking about your brand. The brand personality is important because it deals with your communication with customers! Customers or clients are able to relate to the traits that your brand possesses. There are five main types of brand personalities, excitement, sincerity, ruggedness, competence, and sophistication. An example of a sincere brand would be Disney or Hallmark. An exciting brand would be Nike or Red Bull. A competent brand would be Google and Microsoft. Sophistication would be branded like Tiffany & Co. or Rolex. A rugged brand would be Harley Davidson or Jeep. Julie's brand would certainly fall under the sophisticated branding, with her Julie K ARTelier, the look and feel is all about elegance!

Julie took all of this into consideration when building her own brand image, and urges that everyone also put a lot of thought into how you present your brand to the world. You have to dig deeper than just the brand concept. Do you have a website? What is your social media presence like? Is there a sense of trust and loyalty in the online community that you are building? Julie is a firm believer in building relationships at the manicure table. It is important for her to keep those relationships professional because the experience she receives, as a result, is priceless! Her advice for others is to always take the best photos you can and take advantage of the online world where visual representation is the most important factor in attracting the target audience's attention.

Social media is extremely important as it allows you to reach, nurture and engage with your target market. Social media is more relevant than ever before. With instant access and sharing capabilities, social media marketing blows cold call sales out of the water. Utilizing social media marketing enables you to communicate faster, more often, and with greater relevance. According to Julie, one mistake many make is having one account for professional and personal use. Building a powerful brand out of yourself is something that Julie insists needs to be accomplished by having a separate professional social media account. Doing otherwise - mixing too much professional with business would most likely just cause confusion and a weaker overall professional representation online. Personally, I am not the best with social media. It took me some time to get onto social media other than for my brand, and even then it was not really for me. I realized I needed to hire a social media manager. I knew that my skills were not up to par to have a successful social media marketing plan, so I hired someone to do it for me! This has been a huge game-changer for me, and I have learned so much! They say a picture is worth a thousand words. Pictures on social media showcase your brand!

The next step, expanding your brand, is extremely exciting, yet super nerve-racking at the same time! There are a few reasons why brands expand their market starting with satisfying existing customers' needs. One reason could be that your current target audience isn't doing as well as you had hoped; refocusing your target audience can help. Another is good old competition. By expanding into new markets it could level them to their competitors who may have already been in this market. Here are some steps to take in order to expand into a new market:

1. **Look at your current target audience and business model** - look for areas of improvement.
2. **Write down your goals** - think about your one, three, five to ten year goals for your brand; review your mission and vision statements to help your goals.
3. **Research** - look into competitor markets and product related markets.
4. **Pick your new market** - after thoroughly researching, it is time to choose what market best aligns with your goals.
5. **Feedback with your current market** - this would be a great time to reach out to your existing clients and see what they are looking for from you. Sending emails or questionnaires would be a great way to find out what else your clients want to see from you.
6. **Establish a budget and business plan** - it's time to dive into your new chosen market, but be sure you have a set budget and plan in place, along with a time frame to measure your success.

With strong branding and a successful social media marketing plan, customer loyalty can be built as a foundation for expansion. Branding is the primary reason for loyalty between clients and consumers; whether they only purchase products based on their ingredient list or based on what the brand posts on social media. Branding is a ginormous umbrella, and there are countless things you can do to create client loyalty!

I, Karen, want to share a story that happened a few years ago. The vendors you use should help brand your salon or spa. The level of education is also imperative for your staff to wow clients. Make sure your vendors are supplying you with plenty of education. Years ago, I was talking to the owner of our vendor we used at the time. We were discussing the business, education and leadership programs. I was stunned when he said "I have been in this industry 50 years and there is nothing new to learn, educators just spin the education differently." I was so disappointed to hear his opinion. Two weeks later, his son stopped by the salon and I asked him if he had any new ideas on advertising or branding. His idea was to go to the local highschool and seek out the king and queen, or most popular guy and girl, in school and give them makeovers. He thought, in doing this, everyone will want to follow. I thought this was the stupidest idea. However, I went home and asked my daughter and her friends who were seniors in highschool at the time. After they were done laughing at me, she said this is not the 1970's. After thinking this through, I realized I outgrew the vendor I was using. I chose a different product line and vendor. I couldn't be happier with my decision. They focus on education which is very important to me.

CHAPTER 9:

TO LEADERSHIP, SUCCESS AND BEYOND

Barbara Guillaume

For Barbara, her first glimpse into the world of beauty and fashion came at a young age when she started her successful modeling career in her home city of Paris. As a model, she was fortunate enough to learn about color theory, skin, makeup, and hair from the best beauty pros in the business. It is this well-rounded expertise that has made her one of the most in-demand groomers with a client list including Milo Ventimiglia, Leonardo DiCaprio, Edgar Ramirez, and Tom Hanks. Barbara worked very hard to get where she is today. She radiates perseverance, with an internal drive that keeps her focused on her end goals. In order to work with celebrities, you need to be hired by an agency. Despite getting fired from her first make-up agency, she was still motivated to keep pushing. Her commitment to her passion allowed her to be fully immersed in the beauty world as a make-up artist and groomer, and she fell in love with it. Not only did she pick a niche and put all of her focus there, but she also made sure the specialty she chose aligned with her communication strengths. Men were more open to her than women, so Barbara had to make sure to hone in on her communication skills.

During Barbara's interview, she brings up that anyone can be good at their job, but it's personality that matters in the beauty industry. She talks in depth about how in the beginning of her career she had to mold herself around her clients' personalities and as time passed, eventually she found clients that matched her energy. When it comes to building a clientele, your energy and leadership play a big role. Barbara's best advice when it comes to this is knowing your place, try to be easy going, fun to be around, and mold yourself to your clients in the beginning. Her target audience was clients that were drawn to this simplistic approach. Her belief, which is reflected in her unique-selling point, is that beauty is radiated from the inside out. Barbara also touches base on the fact that she put in the work, time and energy. Even if it didn't necessarily match up with her idea of what it should look like; because she knew it was part of navigating through the process.

Every next level demands change, which sometimes is hard. One of the worst and best decisions that Barbara made in her career was deciding to change agents. You never want to hurt anyone's feelings; however, we do have to stop and ask ourselves "where am I going from here?" "Can I be more?" For Barbara, it's important for her agent to be a "killer" when it comes to finding the best rates, good at communication, and on top of travel. You can't doubt that your agent isn't getting you the best rates; it's important to trust that they have your best interest at hand. Communication is a must. It's important for your agent to be on top of your work from simple things like knowing overtime hours on a job to knowing where you see your career going in the future. Lastly, travel is huge. Are they booking your flights, cars and hotels? Do they know your schedule? It's such a big part of Barbara's career. For Barbara, not only are these the main things that her career runs on, but also her agent is what navigates her future plans and dreams.

One of Babara's greatest moments in her career is when she finally got to the point where she could look at her calendar and say "Oh, wow I'm fully booked." This exact moment is what she had prayed for; it's one of her favorite feelings in her career. Business seems like it comes naturally for Barbara. Her biggest drive to becoming successful with business is her son. She knew she had to do whatever it took to reach a place of spirituality, good energy and success. Business slowed down during the pandemic, which allowed Barbara plenty of time to see what could be next. Next up on the list of dreams is formulating her own facial oil. Knowing that it's a lot to hire a whole team, finding a space to rent, and products in the beginning, Barbara and her business partner started this right in her kitchen. Assembly line and all.

"Leadership is about making others better as a result of your presence and making sure that impact lasts in your absence." -unknown

I, Karen, truly believe that other women were threatened by Barbara's natural beauty! In knowing her place, Barbara had to decide what type of relationship she was going to have with her clients. She realized early on that communicating with each client was different. Therefore, communication was a soft skill that was imperative to Barbara's craft. Barbara understands her place on set, as she is empathetic, so she cares deeply about the overall vibe being right. This allowed her clients to be extremely comfortable working with her. If you aren't sure what your communication style is, you could give our assessment a shot. I used to be a terrible communicator with my staff. I used to walk through my salon and spa and give people jobs where I saw fit; pick some things up here, put this there, do this, etc. I would go back to my office and feel as if I got a lot accomplished, but I pissed off a lot of people by leading that way. It wasn't until I took a leadership course with *Empowering You*, that I discovered my own communication style, and what needed to be changed in order to communicate with my staff better and be more effective. I was able to take my new knowledge back to my staff and we did one communication exercise together! This completely changed the way I communicated and led the whole staff! My communication style, and skills, were totally opposite of my staff. This was a huge game-changer for me!

During the pandemic, all productions, of movies and concerts, shut down for a time being, so Barbara started to question herself and if she wanted to continue being a professional groomer. She didn't have a backup plan, but was resourceful enough to start a brand new company, CIRCA 1970 Luxury Face Oil. She curated a small business, keeping it cost-efficient, doing all marketing and PR herself, and launched. This took leadership skills as well! There are various types of leadership styles, mainly stemming from these 5 styles:

1. Authoritarian Leadership - allows leaders to impose expectations and define outcomes.
2. Participative Leadership - involves team members in the decision-making process.
3. Delegative Leadership - focuses on delegating initiative to team members.
4. Transactional Leadership - leader sets clear goals and rewards for getting the job done.
5. Transformational Leadership - inspires a team with a vision and constantly encourages them to achieve it.

There are of course advantages and disadvantages to all leadership styles, although it is important to find out what leadership style you have to better communicate and lead your team!

Authoritarian Leadership Advantages

- The chain of command is emphasized
- Creates consistent results

Authoritarian Leadership Disadvantages:

- Group input and collaboration reduces
- Strict leadership can sometimes drive employee rebellion

Participative Leadership Advantages:

- Helps with the creation of a strong team
- Increases employee motivation and job satisfaction

Participative Leadership Disadvantages:

- Security issues could arise due to transparency in information sharing
- Communication failures can sometimes happen

Delegative Leadership Advantages:

- Creates a positive work environment
- Innovation and creativity are highly valued

Delegative Leadership Disadvantages:

- Command responsibility is not properly defined
- Creates difficulty in adapting to change

Transactional Leadership Advantages:

- Eliminates or minimizes confusion within the chain of command
- Employee motivation and productivity increases

Transactional Leadership Disadvantages:

- Innovation and creativity is minimized
- Creates more followers rather than leaders among employees

Transformational Leadership Advantages:

- This leads to lower employee turnover rate
- Places high value on company mission/vision

Transformational Leadership Disadvantages:

- Constant motivation and feedback may be required by employees
- This can sometimes lead to the deviation of protocols and regulations

There are four types of communication styles: Dominate, Influencer, Conscientious and Analyzer. What is your communication style? Do you like communicating with lots of data, or do you prefer to focus on feelings?

Please take this short assessment. This is a small sample of one of the Empowering You assessments. Please circle the best answer that describes you.

1) When I am in a meeting, I prefer to sit...

A. At the head of the table
B. Where people can see me
C. Directly next to another person
D. With at least one seat between me and the next person

2) When I speak with a person, I...

A. Look directly at him or her the entire time
B. Look at him or her often
C. Look down sometimes
D. Tend to look around the room more than at the person

3) When I greet people I know fairly well, I...

A. Give them a firm handshake
B. Give them an enthusiastic handshake
C. Give them a hug
D. Say hello but do not touch them

4) When I am talking to people, I...

A. Get annoyed when they stand too close

B. Like to stand close to them

C. Don't mind if they are close to me

D. Feel uncomfortable if they stand too close

5) When other people talk, I...

A. Look for the main point

B. Look for a good story

C. Try to figure out their feelings

D. Look for supporting facts

If you circled mostly A, Dominate

If you circled mostly B, Influencer

If you circled mostly C, Conscientious

If you circled mostly D, Analyser

	Dominate	Influencer	Conscientious	Analyzer
Talking	Gets to the point	Tells good stories	Doesn't offer opinions	Precise
Listening	Poor listener	Doesn't hear details	Sympathetic listener	Seeks facts
Handshake	Firm	Enthusiastic	Gentle	Brief
Personal space	Maintains distance	Likes to be close	Likes hugging	Avoids touching
Movement	Bold	Quick	Slow	Controlled
Workspace	Suggests power	Cluttered	Displays photos	Organized

Leadership and communication are two pillars, but should not be kept separate. Leadership is all about communicating; how and what you communicate to your staff, doing it in an effective way, and feedback from staff. The key to great leadership is clear communication, plain and simple! With the right niche decision, you can direct that personalization to all parts of your business.

CHAPTER 10:
STEADY GROWTH

Niki Levengood & Dottie Greene

Niki and Dottie are connected... not by blood, but by a bond that was created of their own volition.

Niki knew hairstyling was something that came naturally to her. She started her career during her junior and senior years of high school in the cosmetology program. She completed the program. After one year of employment in a chain salon, Niki was promoted to a managerial position, which was a goal of hers. She was a single, full-time working mother. She wanted to spend time with her child while also growing her brand and perfecting her craft. She knew that she wanted to be more attentive to her son's needs, which meant she wanted to spend less time away from him. However, she also wanted to do this while maximizing her working hours. These goals are what lead her to decide to leave a small salon and change direction by building her own business. While establishing her business, she created a space that was more fitting for her child and then her clients' children; which was unusual in her profession.

Niki is certainly an innovator. When you are your own boss, you get to make the rules.

Niki's second passion when it comes to business is being just as compassionate to her team members as she is with her clients. She describes herself as "free spirited and uninhibited." She loves helping women surface their inner beauty and confidence. Niki says, "Looks are everything. If you look good, you feel good." Niki owns two successful salons: Tame Salon located in Ohio and the other in Colorado. That's not all; she also owns a clothing brand called Tame Label, an exclusive hair extension line called Untamed Extensions, and a party rental company called Blush Party Rentals. She's in the process of developing a cosmetic line called Tame Cosmetics. She does whatever she can to help women look their best, and as a result, feel their best. When it comes to her employees, one of Niki's main goals is creating a positive work environment for her stylists. She wants to make sure that everyone feels welcome and actually looks forward to coming to work.

When asked what was her most bizarre moment in her career, Niki told us a story about some former team members. After working at Tame for only a week, this team member came back from his lunch break visibly intoxicated. Niki pulled him to the side and said, "You need to sober up, and when you're feeling better, you need to leave." By doing the right thing and allowing him to stay at the salon to sober up, his behavior escalated and he became angry and verbally abusive, spewing racial slurs at Niki. He was asked to leave the salon immediately. As he left, he chose to further cause a scene by attempting to spit on Niki. Imagine the audacity and disrespect... Thankfully, another team member was able to intervene, and while leaving he still had the energy to hit her car with his belongings. She realized at that point she could not help everyone, but only the ones who truly wanted the help.

Niki notes that she didn't want her team to feel like they have to start their career by receiving less money because they are new to the industry. "I don't want my team to go through the same things that I had to go through," she said. Understanding the struggles of starting in the beauty industry, she treats her team how she wishes she was treated. With that said, she learned the importance of being a good leader and helped her brand grow. Throughout the years, Niki's team has taught her valuable lessons. All of her commitments, relationships, and trial and errors has led her to become who she is today — a badass girl boss. She loves watching her team excel and her business grow. Niki said, "If you have the ability to make someone's life easier, why not help them?" If everyone thought like Niki, the world would be a better place.

Something that really caught my attention regarding Niki was another story about one of her team members. "One of my stylists was moving and didn't want to get a new job, so I decided to open a Tame Salon in Colorado and let her manage it," Niki said. Allowing her to manage a brand-new business where she has the tools, procedures, and processes in place created opportunities for her employees to thrive and grow within the industry. This is similar to franchising a business. We will give you more information on franchising later in the chapter. Niki knew this team member would be a strong manager and was confident that she would do an amazing job. Niki believes employees who feel appreciated are higher performers and will go above and beyond role expectations.

Dottie is a 23-year-old hairstylist at Tame Salon owned by Niki in Columbus, Ohio. Dottie, too, felt drawn to the beauty industry. At the age of five, she would play with her brother's hair and later in life realized that was her calling. She was born into a military family which meant she was always moving around and living in different areas of the country. Before she moved to Columbus, she was living in Washington D.C. In 2018, she decided to move to Columbus to pursue her hairstyling career. She attended the Aveda Institute in Columbus. Being an introvert, Dottie had to learn how to put herself out there and seize any opportunities that came her way. "Whatever I have to do, I'm going to do it," Dottie said. Stepping out of her comfort zone, she started introducing herself to the staff and different people at hair shows, which allowed her to create connections that would last a lifetime. Both Niki and Dottie discussed how learning is a continuous process. You don't just go to school, graduate, and instantly know everything there is to know about hair. You learn new skills, techniques, and solutions *every single day.*

At the Aveda Institute in Columbus, Dottie became more interested and drawn to editorial work. She loves the creativity involved in these looks and the fact that stylists inspire others to be creative. The first time she ever heard about the North American Hairstyling Awards (NAHA) was during her time at the Aveda school. As soon as she heard about this coveted award ceremony, she went home and wrote it down as one of her goals to accomplish. At first, she was unaware that students were allowed to enter the competition. A few months went by and the NAHA competition was coming up. Her instructors and classmates at school encouraged her to enter. Dottie decided to go for it; after all, it was on her list of goals to accomplish. She was chosen to be the student representing Aveda Columbus. She spent three days creating her editorial looks to be submitted for the competition. To get the perfect photos of the look she created, Dottie teamed up with Keith Bryce, an editorial photographer and hairdresser. "It was a lot of work, but it was so fulfilling," she said. After she submitted her looks, she had to wait *months* to find out that she was a finalist. This meant that she would be attending the NAHA awards ceremony in Long Beach, California. To get this far was a huge accomplishment.

Before packing up and traveling to a different state, Dottie prepared a speech just in case she won. "I wrote it down like 100 times on the plane ride there," she said. She said that she didn't want to get too excited and then be let down. Her nerves were really kicking in because she wasn't the best public speaker. When she arrived at the awards ceremony, she walked down the red carpet and saw several beauty industry icons, such as Geno Stampora, Chrystofer Benson, Philip Wolff, and Elizabeth Faye. Dottie was right there with them. The nerves that she had prior to the event were a testament to how badly she wanted to win this award. Dottie won the NAHA award, and that was a *huge* accomplishment.

Hearing about Dottie's huge success, it's important to note that she did and still does face serious challenges. Dottie underwent two hip surgeries after graduating high school and before attending beauty school. The first two surgeries didn't halt her pain completely, but that didn't stop her from deciding to go after her dreams and attend hair school. Nor did it stop her from moving to Columbus to pursue her cosmetology license at The Aveda School in Columbus. This taught Dottie the ins and outs of hairstyling. She would tell herself, *Focus on the dream, not the pain.* This was her mantra and she would say it to herself over and over when struggling to be on her feet all day. During the pandemic, she had to take another year off to get two more failed hip surgeries. Shortly after, she had to have two hip replacements. These challenges have been hard for Dottie, but she tries to keep her head up and face them with grace. Even though she still experiences pain daily, she never let this discourage her from accomplishing her dreams and striving to reach her goals. Many people suggest she choose a different career that doesn't require her to be on her feet. She immediately disregards their advice because she KNOWS she was destined to be a hairstylist.

"I know this is what I'm meant to do, and I will never let anything stop me from pursuing and achieving my dreams and goals. As long as I'm alive, I'm going to be doing hair," she said.

As I mentioned earlier, I would like to give you a little information regarding franchising. But first, let's do an assessment. On a separate sheet of paper, please answer the questions below. Be as honest and use as much detail as possible when answering.

1. What are your reasons for wanting to own a franchise?
    a. Is it for the money?

    b.   Is it to be your own boss?

    c.   Is it to make your own schedule?

    d.   Is it because you're bored with your current career?

2. Are you driven by financial earnings?

    a.   Would you like to make more money than you are presently?

3. Do you mesh well in the corporate environment?

    a.   Do you enjoy having a boss?

    b.   Have you ever been referred to as a "rebel"?

4. Do you enjoy working hard, even if the reward seems distant?

5. Are you independent?

    a.   Do you seize initiative?

    b.   Do you wait for others to take a leadership role?

    c.   Do you seek others' approval before making a decision?

6. Are you a risk taker?

7. Do you generally have a positive outlook toward your endeavors?

8. Do you consider yourself to be a "people person"?

    a.   Are your interactions with others effective?

    b.   Do you find that you like others?

9. Can you abide with a system that is already in place?

    a.   Do you have to have everything your way?

10. Do you enjoy teaching and coaching?

    a.   Do you take pleasure in training and supporting others in new tasks?

Now that you've finished your assessment, let's talk about franchising.

A franchise is a type of license that grants a franchisee access to a franchisor's proprietary business knowledge, processes, and trademarks; thus, allowing the franchisee to sell a product or service under the franchisor's business name. For a company, it's an opportunity to accelerate their growth with limited investment and involvement in day to day operations. For it to work, you (the franchisee) would pay an initial investment fee, followed by regular royalty payments to the company (the franchiser). This is a highly monitored market, and resources such as the International Franchise Association (IFA) are available for both the support and protection of investors. Some things that are included in franchising are: training, policies, license, limited period, marketing support, technology support, and royalty. When considering franchising a company, you should take into consideration:

- How much will you need to cover the initial startup fees (I.E. equipment, licensing, real estate, etc.)?
- How much liquid capital do you need to maintain to cover the franchise until you break even or see a positive return on investment?
- What are the ongoing franchise fees?
- What are the royalty expectations?

Some benefits of buying a franchise are:

1. You can skip the line: purchasing a franchise allows entrepreneurs to circumvent the many challenges of establishing a new business from the ground up — a key benefit which frequently attracts new entrepreneurs to this business model. By buying into an established company, investors skip over challenges, such as, creating a business plan, projecting profitability, creating a go-to market strategy, naming the business, and trademarking.

2. No need for market research: before offering the opportunity for a new reseller to join their model, franchisers conduct extensive market research to determine whether there is adequate demand for business in that location. Straight away, this eliminates the need for you to perform your own in-depth independent studies on the potential and consumer appetite of this venture.

3. Operational Guidance: besides a business model, franchising offers ongoing profitability and functional supervision; thus, providing the necessary support you'll need. This is important to navigate consumer, industry, or economic challenges which may arise along the way.

4. Ready-made Branding and Marketing: having access to an established brand helps achieve instant profitability; while operating under the same branding, you will continue to benefit from all past and present marketing and advertising run by the franchiser. In addition to this, your franchisor will support your marketing and advertising, with guidance to content creation, campaign delivery, demographic targeting, market analysis, and success metrics. This significantly reduces the time and resources needed to invest in this area, allowing you to focus on operational matters and their impact on the business.

5. An Existing Customer Base: on top of gaining the rights to operate under a known brand, franchise investors also have access to something arguably even more valuable: customer loyalty.

6. Access to Support Tools and Training: sophisticated online tools and software systems will be made available to you as part of your investment, allowing you to maintain the consistency of the franchise's overall offering (such as its customer service, reputation, market share, and profitability). Knowing how the point of sale and customer retention system works, staff will not be weighed down with these administrative duties.

7. Reduced Overall Risk: statistics show that over 50% of start-ups fail in the first five years of operation, with that figure rising to 70% over ten years. Franchises are not bulletproof, but there is more security and guidance available through a franchise model.

Franchising does come with downsides, such as:

1. Initial acquisition fee.
2. Creative control is limited.
3. Freedom when it comes to operations.
4. Product offering, marketing strategy and branding strategy are pre-determined by the franchiser and cannot be adjusted when you want.

After reading this chapter, I hope you have a general understanding of what a franchise is and how it works. Also, I hope you are more informed to either start your own business from scratch or invest in a franchise. If you currently own a business, is franchising something you considered?

CHAPTER 11:

YOUR NICHE IS YOUR PITCH

Ruth Roche

R uth Roche is a seven time North American Hairstyling Awards (NAHA) winner. She comes from a family of engineers. Even with this fact in mind, she was still unsure about what to go to college for. She ended up following in her family's footsteps and attending UCSB (University Of California Santa Barbara) for mechanical engineering. During her time in college, she was cutting her friend's hair in exchange for a 6-pack of beer (typical college student). Ruth and her friends would visit a local bar and when she used the soap in the bathroom, it reminded her of a product that was used in her hair at the salon. Every time she would wash her hands with this soap, she would have a vision of her working at a salon. Eventually, Ruth decided that she didn't really want to be an engineer. Contrary to what her parents wanted for her, she decided to drop out of college and go to hair school. Ruth started cosmetology school in LA, but decided to transfer back to Santa Barbara where she had already lived and attended college years prior.

After she graduated from cosmetology school in Santa Barbara, she started apprentice training at Apace, the best salon in Santa Barbara. She was on the floor at this salon for three years until she was ready for her next venture. At the time, Trevor Sorbie, who is an icon in the hair industry, was starting his first U.S. artistic team and was holding auditions. Ruth really wanted to have the opportunity to work with Trevor, so she decided to try out.

There were over 300 other hairstylists who had the same idea, but only 12 of them were going to be chosen for the artistic team. Trevor actually only ended up picking three candidates, and Ruth was one of them. It was such an accomplishment for Ruth to be able to stand out from 300 people who were just as, if not more, talented than she was. Ruth even told us herself that she was a terrible hairdresser at this time.

"He only picked me because I had guts. I went for it and just didn't care," Ruth said.

Trevor ended up taking her under his wing. He trained her so that her skills were on the same level as her desire for greatness. When Ruth found out that she made the team, her mother was there to congratulate her and share her accomplishments. Unfortunately, Ruth's mother was unwell at the time and passed away before she had the chance to see Ruth start training with Trevor and become who she is today. Even though it was extremely heartbreaking when Ruth's mother passed, she said it gave her the motivation she needed to dive head first into her craft. "I don't think I would be where I am today if my mother hadn't died at that specific time in my life," Ruth said. Ruth noted this as the defining moment in her career. She was able to put the vices aside and focus wholeheartedly on her career in the beauty industry.

Ruth said that training with Trevor Sorbie was one of the hardest things she had ever done. He was extremely hard on her. Trevor would randomly test her in the middle of training with Vivienne Mackinder, his artistic director at the time. When the training was complete, Ruth was teaching five days a week in the advanced section. This was when Ruth moved to Chicago to teach at Pivot Point. This opportunity was offered to Ruth just six months in, and she decided to take a chance and move to a different state. Ruth loved her new job, and her favorite part was seeing her students get the "lightbulb moment." She knew that her calling was to help others learn by sharing new things with them.

Ruth's life might have seemed like it was all sunshine and rainbows, but she was still trying to find herself and was not truly happy. She decided to relocate to Washington after she saw how happy her friend was there. She traveled two or three times a month, and this was when her career started to take off. After living in Washington for six months, she thought to herself, *I have to get the hell out of here.* A woman named Mary Brunetti offered Ruth a job at her salon in Long Island and she felt this was her chance to leave Washington. She loved living in New York and stayed there for five years. Opportunities kept presenting themselves to Ruth. Trevor asked her if she wanted to move to London, but she decided not to because she wanted to be an "American hero." A lot of the top hairstylists are from the UK, and she wanted to stay in the U.S. to show people that they can be successful here as well.

Ruth started talking to Redken, and they offered her the position of global artistic director. Before accepting the offer, she consulted with Trevor, who said it was a great opportunity. After working as the Redken Global Artistic Director for five years, Ruth decided to take a break and build her brand. Ruth Ann Roche Educational Productions (RARE) was an advanced academy. Unfortunately, she went into business with someone who was dishonest. Ruth trusted this person and had to rewrite all the curriculum when she discovered the person's true nature. Although this was a major setback, Ruth didn't let it stop her from releasing the RARE academy.

Another discouraging situation happened when Ruth was trying to find a location for her studio. There was a lot of realty available in New York, but the realtors would talk to her like she was stupid. They would "mansplain" realty as if she had no clue what she was doing. Discouraged for the second time, Ruth stopped seeking out a place for her salon. She threw her hands up in the air and said, "Screw it, I'll just focus on the academy!" While on a walk one day, Ruth saw a for rent sign on a beautiful space. She called the number and started talking with a woman who was also named Ruth. She eventually found the perfect location for the studio. It was on the first floor, had a huge storefront, and lofted ceilings. RARE, Ruth's salon, was perfect. The shop was unique in the sense that she only hired stylists from school. She loved education and enjoyed teaching from the ground up. The interview process was long, but Ruth said that it was helpful because it weeded out people who didn't want to put the work in.

Ruth didn't have a huge clientele at her first salon because she was focused on teaching at the time. She decided it was a good idea to collaborate with someone in hopes to grow her client base. Her new colleague was a colorist, but their relationship didn't last long due to their differences. This was another hard situation for Ruth because she truly wanted it to work out.

During all the hustle and bustle of running her salon, Ruth got an agent in New York. She worked with celebrities such as Anne Hathaway, Mariah Carey, Lindsay Lohan, Sheryl Crow, Kelly Ripa, and many others. Fashion and doing everything she has always dreamed of played a big role. She loved being able to see something in her head and figure out how to make it a reality. Even though she loved what she was doing, she started to burn out. Ruth decided it would be best if she sold her salon, so she did. Prior to selling her salon to one of her employees at the time, she got a new job with Pureology as their artistic director. At this time, she kept a small clientele because she traveled frequently. Ruth worked as the co-artistic director with Wendy Belanger for nine years. She eventually decided to return to Redken — they never lost contact with each other and this was a great network for her to be part of. It was also upon her return to Redken that Ruth really focused on building an online presence.

One of the most memorable moments for Ruth was when she was on stage with Daniel, one of Trevor's assistants, with an audience of 400 people and a person started loudly asking several people in the audience questions. A gentleman, who was in the audience earlier that day, was asking the people if anyone found any keys. Then he started screaming, "I lost my keys." "Did anyone find keys?" Daniel called him to come closer to the stage so he could hear what he was saying. Daniel said, "let me see if I can help you." Daniel asked the audience to get up from their chairs and look for the keys. What an ice breaker when you're onstage, three shows a day, with an audience that big. The keys were found and it turned out to be a great laugh.

Ruth offered some advice that she got from her mentor, Trevor. He told her to focus on her craft, stay humble, and help others achieve their dreams. You can't go wrong this way. Another piece of advice is to do your research before starting a business. It's important to learn about business and how to run one before you go in blindly.

Ruth said people tried to tell her this, but she disregarded their warnings and ended up learning the hard way. Owning a business is not for everyone, so make sure you know exactly what you're getting into. When it comes to building clientele, Ruth urges the stylists of today to put their phones down and focus on the client. All conversation should be about your client and their hair; they shouldn't have to compete with a cell phone for your attention. Show your clients that you care about them and how they feel. It's also important to ask for referrals and build lasting relationships. A line that always worked for Ruth is: "I think you're really cool, and I would love to have more clients like you!"

Ruth was extremely lucky she found her niche and a place where she would fit in pretty easily. A lot of this was because Ruth took a chance outside of her comfort zone. There are many people who struggle and take years to find their right niche. Right from the start, you should save yourself years of moaning and groaning of not fitting in by taking the time to really figure it out at the beginning. One of the most important things you can do to succeed in a business is to find your profitable niche. A niche is a specialized segment of the market for a particular kind of product or service. A good niche appeals to a specific group or solves a specific problem. It has to align with your talent, skills, and values. It is also something that should be planned and thoroughly researched. A good niche is carefully crafted and highly focused.

The beauty industry offers so many job opportunities which can be overwhelming. I would like to help you narrow down your niche. The next exercise will help you narrow it down and give you some clarity. Please answer the following questions in as much detail as possible on a separate piece of paper.

1. What are your interests and passions?
2. What problems drive you crazy?
3. What problems can you solve?
4. What is your unique approach to problem solving?
5. What is your unique selling point?
6. What are three adjectives people use the most when describing you?
7. What are your top three values?
8. What accomplishments are you most proud of?
9. How will you determine the profitability of your niche?
10. Test your idea. What are your results?

There is no perfect process to finding your niche. You want to go through the steps, but you don't want to get stuck in the planning stage. Taking some action is necessary when narrowing down your niche. Many people have to step outside of their comfort zone in order to do this. They say when you're outside your comfort zone that's when you're taking on bigger challenges for a bigger result. When you step outside of your comfort zone, not only will you benefit by accelerating your business growth, but your personal growth will improve as well.

Please answer the questions below (how you currently feel in your career):

1. What are three activities inside of your comfort zone?
2. What are three activities outside of your comfort zone?
3. What is one activity outside of your comfort zone that you could carry out for a week?

CHAPTER 12:

MATH IS MONEY, MONEY IS FUN

Susie Carder

Building a business is not easy. Especially when you are building a business, and yourself, from scratch. Susie Carder, profit coach, and self-made millionaire started with one salon and health spa and was able to turn it into one of the most successful businesses in the country! She then founded and sold three profitable companies, the last of which sold for eight figures to Cengage, which is a company that sells e-textbooks and online homework. However, that's not really where her success all started. Susie's journey in the beauty industry can be traced all the way to her college days in 1982. Like many others in previous chapters, she was stuck in college with no true passion or direction of what her future would be. She knew she had the passion and the drive, she just didn't know what for. One thing she knew is that she hated college. Susie's aunt encouraged her to start this new journey in the beauty industry. They were gardening, and immediately after her aunt suggested this new career path, they got dressed and headed to the nearest beauty school. She signed up and instantly knew this was her home. She finally felt like she belonged instead of just going through the motions. From this day forward,

Susie fell head over heels in love with the industry, the art behind it, and the clients within that line of work.

Of course, back then she didn't really think that she would be where she is today. Susie has guided hundreds of companies to develop personalized operation systems in finance, sales, and marketing. As an international speaker, Susie's spit-fire personality, sharp wit, and heart-warming stories are beautifully woven in with her decades of business knowledge to educate and compel audiences towards financial freedom. Susie Carder is a globally recognized profit coach and inventor of the Predictable Success Method™. She has built two 10 million dollar businesses that she later sold. She currently owns her 10th company. Susie Carder's consulting company, also another multi million dollar business, focuses on building seven figure businesses around the world. She is the author of nine books and multiple training programs. Her Best-Selling book, Power Your Profits: How to Take Your Business From $10,000 to $10 Million, is available today. Back when she first started, she was just happy that she found her calling and felt blessed to be able to do something she truly loved. Susie notes that none of her success could have come to fruition without the motivation and encouragement she received from her clients. She attributes a lot of her accomplishments to the people that pushed her to do more and share her talents with the world.

But Susie didn't always have the mindset needed to accomplish all of that and break the glass ceilings of the beauty industry coaching. She traces her turning point back when she got divorced from someone she considered the love of her life. With the divorce came financial hardship. Susie had to figure out how to support herself and her two children without help from her ex-husband or her family. She describes this desire for her children to have a good life as her first "why." "I was on a journey of desperation," Susie says. Channeling all of that pain and disappointment into her work forced her to kick into survival mode. She used the skills she learned in beauty school to support her and her children, and soon she was making a quarter of a million dollars per year! Her hyperfocus on work allowed her to reach this level of income just by being a hairdresser, but it also took away her ability to look at the bigger picture. It wasn't until people began asking her, how the hell are you making so much money from hairdressing? At this point, Susie was not paying attention to anyone else. She was focused on her goals and staying in her own lane. Susie says that when she finally "looked up," her rep asked if she would be interested in teaching some of the salons and spas to become as successful as she had. What had started as just a few training sessions here and there quickly turned into her clients requesting that she provide more tools for them to create profitable businesses. She started getting more and more offers to teach workshops and give speeches. She was reluctant at first, unable to see what others were seeing in her success. Teaching opportunities slowly turned to encouragement to write her own book. After her first book became a bestseller, she knew that she had stepped up her game to a whole new level. It was time to act on it. Her mindset was shifted.

Let's take a look at your own mindset by completing the assessment below. From 1 to 10, rate your mental readiness (with 1 being the worst, 10 being the best, and 5 being in the middle). Be sure to answer these questions honestly. You are the only person holding yourself back!

I am...

1. **Committed to letting the struggles go**
2. **Clear on what my life purpose is**
3. **Managing your ups and downs**
4. **Comfortable with change**
5. **Free from the past**
6. **Conscientious of my limiting beliefs**
7. **Aware of what stops my success**

8. **Engage in ongoing personal development**
9. **Maintaining healthy boundaries**
10. **Coachable, not committed to being a lone ranger**

Susie knew that adopting the right mindset was only the beginning. She still lacked the skills necessary to scale her income to what it is today. By this time, Susie says that her clients were her biggest motivating factor. She had made enough money to support herself and her children, and now was being asked to help others do the same thing. They pushed her to create more materials that could help them see financial growth. This was another one of her "why's." When approached about pricing, she would usually just ask: "How much are you willing to pay for it?" Her expertise in financial literacy was only just birthing what she has today. Her success with writing a book and watching the impact of her coaching resulted in her becoming more focused on and passionate about helping other business owners achieve what came naturally to her – growth and sustainability.

When Susie sold her company for millions in 2005, she thought she would never have to work again. She started investing in the real estate and stock markets to diversify her portfolio. Everything was going well until the market crash of 2008. Susie's bank account took a significant hit. In one day, she had lost 90% of her wealth. Before she knew it, she was spiraling trying to think about how she was going to come back from this. Right as she was about to throw in the towel, she heard a voice in her head telling her to *get up*, and she listened. This situation revealed one of the keys to being successful: *believe in yourself and listen to that inner voice telling you to keep going*. Not only did this situation inspire Susie to listen to her gut feelings, but it emphasized the necessity to have more money in reserve for times like this. She realized that her identity was wrapped in her wealth. Her wealth is what defined her, but when she lost it, she was forced to rebrand herself. Susie tells us that from this point on, rebranding herself was all about strategy.

As she led business after business to success, another test of her talents came unexpectedly. A serious car accident threatened Susie's life and instantly took her away from her business. As she took time off for surgery and healing, something incredible happened behind the scenes. Not only did her business stay afloat, it expanded tenfold. The systems she created enabled her staff to carry on without her. Susie's calling became crystal clear: Bring this level of freedom to others. Susie Carder is a profit coach. She has helped thousands of businesses rise, have radical success strategies, taking them from ordinary to explosive. And when she coaches you, being average or running an average business instantly drops from your list of options. She is relentless in pursuing your goals, comes with a 20-year proven track record, and has two ten million dollar companies under her belt.

Susie has had her ups and downs and shares some characteristics that helped her reach this level of financial success. She says that **transforming your mindset** is one of the most important things. You need to be able to shift your focus on the drop of a dime, and adapt to your surroundings. When she lost 90% of her wealth, she had to adapt and strategize her rebranding in order to rebound from this setback. Another characteristic that Susie describes is **the ability to recreate your "why."** Without her family or husband there for support, she had to find her own reasons to keep going. As we discussed earlier in the chapter, originally Susie's "why" was her children. As she continued to grow in the industry, her "why" changed from her children to her clients who were pushing her to do more. It is this push that created a new reason for her to continue. At the end of the day she loved helping others and sharing her tips for financial success, so she persisted. Lastly, Susie offered up this piece of advice: *you have to be willing to be incredibly uncomfortable.* In order to truly experience growth you have to put yourself out there. Susie labels herself as a trained extrovert. Yes she is a public speaker and talks to people daily, but she was not always like this. Growing up in a big family taught Susie how to hide to avoid getting in trouble. With this new business venture came the necessity to be in the public eye. She was not born with an inherent extroverted personality and had to train herself to be more confident when speaking to large crowds. New doors will not open unless you give yourself a chance to be vulnerable.

Now, let's take a look at your relationship with money. Think about it a little bit. Was it always what it is today? Have you experienced an event in YOUR life that served as a turning point for how you viewed money? Your relationship with money affects your money management because it all stems from the same place. At a younger age, think about what your parents taught you about money and money management. Take a look at yourself today, are there similarities? Relationships with money directly correlate with the nurturing received during childhood about money and values, along with the way you have stored this information in your mind.

Susie's relationship with money changed as she grew older. When she was a child growing up with eight brothers and sisters in a small house, her family didn't have money to spend on anything but the bare necessities. Finances were not an acceptable topic of conversation in their household. There was an unspoken policy of "don't ask because there isn't any" in her family. Her father even said that at the age of 18 they had to either get a job or get married. Growing up, Susie never got an allowance. She was forced to have the attitude of "no one's going to save me" and "if it's meant to be it's up to me." Because of these factors, Susie was always working. At the age of 10, Susie was cleaning houses, babysitting, and doing yard work for money. Working all of these "odd jobs" showed Susie that she had to depend on herself. As you can see, Susie has always been a hustler; in the best way possible. When she got married, she thought that a man was going to "save" her. She soon realized that she shouldn't have depended on someone else for money. When going through the divorce process at 24 years old, Susie had to file for bankruptcy. She received no child support or alimony and was on her own again. Susie felt like she was a loser and was ashamed to be in this position. This was the moment she decided that she never wanted to feel like this again. Susie wanted to have her own money for times like this. After going through these financial hardships, she decided to start doing things differently. Susie's relationship with money went through yet another transformation. She started being more mindful of her credit, and stopped buying things that she couldn't afford. Susie started putting money away for retirement at the age of 25. It's never too early to start saving for your future. This new outlook allowed her to build wealth instead of just shopping to have new things. Being strategic with her financial decisions helped Susie determine how much she could spend and where it should be spent.

When Susie's daughters were old enough to understand money, she wanted to instill the same values that she had surrounding finances. Her children didn't get an allowance without working for it. They had to paint fences, put binders together, and do other tasks in order to receive their weekly allowance. When they got their allowance, they were taught to spend half and save the rest for a rainy day. "You earn it, you keep it!" Susie said. With all of the changes in Susie's relationship with money, she wanted to make one thing clear; "the more you learn, the more you earn." Whether that be learning in school, or just learning how to handle your money more effectively, education and experience are the keys to smart spending.

Susie believes intention and purpose play a vital role in your relationship with money. Your intention is something that you aim and plan for. The purpose is what drives you for something to be done or created. Marrying these two factors births money management skills and the attraction of more opportunities, much like what happened with Susie. Through this book, we have discussed goals, where we want to be, and how to get there. At this time, look at your various goals that are mapped out and the steps you need to take in order to get there. You should look at these goals and understand what needs to be done in order to make it to the next step; whether that means how much money you need to save or make. What is your intention for your future in the beauty industry? What is your purpose?

Many people limit themselves due to not playing big in the world. Limiting yourself means that you may be insecure, afraid, and aren't really sure what you're doing. Don't self-sabotage, be your own cheerleader and stay positive.

There are a few self-limiting things that numerous people do:

- When you think that what is happening to you is out of your control - this is your life and you are in the driver's seat!
- You hide from your problems, or you victimize yourself - take accountability for your actions and life!
- You are resistant to change - take baby steps.
- You aren't investing in yourself, whether that be time, money, or commitment.

Take control of your life and just do it! Do not let self-doubt creep in and wreck what you are working towards. It becomes clear when discussing success in entrepreneurial careers that they will not work out due to the nature of their expectations and how they go about fulfilling them. Removing limitations on yourself requires a completely different mindset. Think about your strengths and passions, make sure that this is still in line with your current goals. Write down and acknowledge what is stopping you. What are conscious efforts that you can make in order to change? Keeping a positive mindset, and feeling positive about yourself is huge in removing limitations on yourself. Have someone close to you be your accountability support, hire a personal coach to help navigate you through your life, and remind yourself that you are a badass!

Setting yourself up for success means you have the foundation to live the life you want, and you have the foundation for having more time, more energy, better relationships, and more money. You need to believe in yourself and have a mental toughness to keep going through the hardships. Continue to write down your goals, the steps needed to accomplish those goals, and the deadline for the goal. You will also need a great support system! When asking for help, not handouts, treat others equitably and fairly, just as you deserve the same. Do not expect something for nothing. Successful professionals realize that if we aren't willing to pay for products and services, then others won't be willing to pay for ours, like karma!

If you take anything away from this book, let it be this: never stop learning. I have said it before and I will say it again, and again, and again! Those who think they know it all truly do not; it doesn't work that way. Those people who know they don't know it all, have worked hard and continue to learn new things all the time. If you haven't done this already, sit down and write down your goals. Where do you want to be in three years? How much money do you want to make in three years? How much money have you saved in three years? These are all questions you should be asking yourself, and more! If you feel like you are in a good spot, think bigger. If you don't feel like you're in a good spot, don't be afraid to ask for help. Help could be a life coach, an accountability partner, an accountant, etc. Look for our companion course, Rags to Riches in Action, where we will cover everything in the book, from a more in-depth point of view and hear from our contributing authors!

Just take some action!

CONCLUSION

Now that we have come to the end of our journey together, it is important to reflect back on every chapter and the vital takeaways from each expert. These are stories of people who actually made it big! You need to dig deep into their stories and ask yourself, how is it possible for me to do the same? Look back at the assessments you did in each chapter and what the lesson takeaways are. Once you know what the lessons are, map out and plan your own journey. As much as it may feel overwhelming, you need to just take-action and you WILL live your dream. Whatever it is, take *some* sort of action. Even picking this book and reading it to the very end is a big step!

I think what a lot of people are missing is confidence. Confidence in themselves and their craft. If you are not confident in your skills, then who will feel confident coming to you for services? You must begin by implementing what you are good at and turning it into a well-oiled machine. After discovering what you are good at, always remember that it is key to listen to yourself and never stop learning. Time and time again I have said this because it's so important! Further your education and never stop learning! Educating yourself and your clients makes a world of difference! Continue learning and taking classes! I have spent over fifty thousand in continuing my own education, and well over one hundred thousand for my staff over the years! First and foremost, be a hard worker, or you will never see your own potential. I always talk about raising the bar; the owner and managers should continue to set goals to keep raising the bar! The minute you think you have made it, is the minute you stop growing and people become lackadaisical and the business starts crumbling.

The beauty industry is forever growing and changing, and you need to keep up with the styles, trends, and education or you will always be chasing to catch up. For example, older stylists may be great but are generally not up to date with the current trends, cuts, styles, and colors. Their end results could possibly look out of date and not trendy.

Once you begin, you have to ensure to create and sustain a good work-life balance. Work-life balance is extremely important to me, and I think that everyone deeply values their time to themselves. Understanding what work-life balance works best for you depends on your needs, wants, and time! Partnerships and owning vs. renting were covered in chapter four. It can either work out really well or really bad; make sure you are getting professional advice and consult with an accountant, lawyer, or bookkeeper. Taking the step from renting to owning is huge; figure out what will work best for you. In chapter five we discussed defining your ideal client. Knowing who your ideal client is, and how to attract and sustain them, will make or break your business.

Creating your dream team is what will take you to the next level! Getting the right people in the door for the job can be hard, and it can be a long process, but it doesn't have to be! Creating codes of conduct, implementing systems, and team building are some ways to attract the right employee for you. Finally, set crystal clear goals and break down each one step by step to accomplish the goal. Make sure you can measure each goal and have a timeline for when each step should be done. Set yourself up for success by planning, setting goals, and working hard! Setting goals for yourself is a great way to step closer to your dreams, all while holding yourself accountable.

Our *Rags to Riches in Action* course is one way you can take-action. We will be teaching you all these lessons covered in this book, in depth and much more! We will have our contributing authors speak on their success, and encourage you to do the same. This is the type of book that can be read over and over again. There is a lot of information covered in each chapter. Therefore, you will have many "Ah-ha" moments.

My end goal was to inspire others in the beauty industry, to swing big, to dream big, and to go after your dreams in this desirable industry! For the most part, you know what you want the next chapter in your life to be. If you don't, you most likely feel bored and over it. There are people who like to stay comfortable, and stay at the level they are. Listen to yourself and your body; in my experience it will let you know when it's time to make a change and transition into the next chapter! Go to Rags to Riches in Action! https://www.iconicriches.com/rags-to-riches-in-action-course to begin the next step in your journey!

ACKNOWLEDGEMENTS

This book would not have been possible without the amazing people in the book. A huge thank you to Drew Schaefering, Aika Flores, Geno Stampora, Amy Carter, Damone Roberts, Kelly Smith, Matthew Collins, Julie Kandalec, Barbara Guillaume, Niki Levengood, Dottie Greene, Ruth Roche and Susie Carder.

Thank you again Susie for being my mentor and coach. Your Global Leadership Program gave me the tools to become an author and develop the Rags to Riches in Action Course. You were always pointing me in the right direction. Thank you for all the times you said "you got this!" Thank you to Mwale & Chantel Henry for showing me how to write a best-selling book, and to Josie Martinez for your marketing genius! Mark Stern, a big thank you for making my media press box one of the coolest boxes ever. And a huge thank you to Jim, my husband, who proofread my chapters several times.

ABOUT THE AUTHOR

Karen Pudetti is a mom first to her two daughters. She graduated with her accounting degree and worked for CPA firms Fortune 500 companies, prior to starting her own business in the beauty industry. She owns a 16,000 square foot building which is home to Luxe Salon Spa and Laser Center.

REFERENCES

1. Adam Hayes, "What Is A Franchise, and How Does It Work?," 2021, https://www.investopedia.com/terms/f/franchise.asp

2. Business Jargons, "Franchising," https://businessjargons.com/franchising.html

3. Efficient Hire, "5 Things To Consider Before Starting A Franchise," 2019, https://www.efficienthire.com/5-factors-to-consider-before-starting-a-franchise/

4. Effy Pafitis, "The 8 Benefits Of Buying a Franchise," 2019, https://www.startingbusiness.com/blog/franchising-benefits

5. Franchise Opportunities Network, "Is Franchising Right For Me? A Self-Survey to Help You Find Out," https://www.franchiseopportunities.com/resources/self-survey

6. Expert Panel, Forbes Coaches Council, "12 Ways To Quickly And Strategically Scale Down Your Business With Minimal Damage," 2019, https://www.forbes.com/sites/forbescoachescouncil/2019/04/30/12-ways-to-quickly-and-strategically-scale-down-your-business-with-minimal-damage/?sh=4b-92dc0f6fc4

7. Stuart Gentle, "Downsizing Without Disruption: A Guide To Scaling Down Your Business," 2021, https://www.onrec.com/news/news-archive/downsizing-without-disruption-a-guide-to-scaling-down-your-business

8. Indeed, "How to Write a Code of Conduct (With Template)," https://www.indeed.com/hire/c/info/write-a-code-of-conduct

9. Advantix, "Top Five Reasons That Salons Fail & How To Avoid It," 2020, https://www.imagiquesalonsuites.com/top-reasons-that-salons-fail/

10. Jeremy Durant, "The Importance Of Knowing Your Ideal Client, 2013, https://www.bopdesign.com/bop-blog/2013/04/the-importance-of-knowing-your-ideal-client/

11. ClientFlow, "33 Ways to Get More Clients," https://clientflow.com/blog/33-ways-to-get-more-clients/

12. Chron Contributor, "Examples Of Branding In Marketing," 2020, https://smallbusiness.chron.com/examples-branding-marketing-11685.html

13. Jennifer Herrity, "4 Steps To Building A Brand," (2021), https://www.indeed.com/career-advice/career-development/steps-to-building-a-brand

14. Go-To Marketing Strategies/Modern Postcard, "Successful Branding: Five Key Elements and One Mantra, https://www.modernpostcard.com/knowledge/articles/successful-branding-five-key-elements-and-one-mantra

15. Lee Froschheiser, "Communication: The most important key to leadership success," https://www.reliableplant.com/Read/12675/communication-most-important-key-to-leadership-success

16. Evan Tarver, "What Is Brand Personality? How It Works and Examples," 2021, https://www.investopedia.com/terms/b/brand-personality.asp

17. Yellow Fishes, "Why Is Brand Personality Important?" 2016, https://medium.com/@theyellowfishes/why-is-brand-personality-important-97e009a0c78

18. Brian Lischer, "The Psychology Of Brand Personality," https://www.ignytebrands.com/the-psychology-of-brand-personality/

19. "How To Find Your Brand Personality," 2021, https://devrix.com/tutorial/how-to-find-your-brand-personality/

20. "Why Social Media Is Important In 2022," https://www.webfx.com/social-media/learn/why-is-social-media-so-important/

21. "8 Reasons Why Social Media Is More Important Than Ever," https://www.brandignity.com/2011/03/4-reasons-why-social-media-is-more-important-than-ever/

22. "History Of Social Media (It's Younger Than You Think)," https://www.broadbandsearch.net/blog/complete-history-social-media

23. Rebecca Battman, "6 Reasons Social Media Can Be Effective For Your Business," https://rbl-brandagency.com/6-reasons-social-media-business/

24. "Top 10 Benefits Of Social Media in the Digital Era," https://digitalmarketinglight.com/social-media-advantages/

25. "Communication Styles Quiz and Assessment," https://www.leadershipiq.com/blogs/leadershipiq/39841409-quiz-whats-your-communication-style

26. Christopher Carter, "Key Documents Needed for the Formation of a Partnership," https://smallbusiness.chron.com/key-documents-needed-formation-partnership-24064.html

27. Susan Ward, "Why Most Business Partnerships Fail," 2020/2022, https://www.thebalancemoney.com/why-business-partnerships-fail-4107045

28. Mercer Smith, "The 4 communication styles and how they impact customer communication," 2020, https://front.com/blog/4-communication-styles

29. Smart Money Moves, "7 Signs You're Failing at Managing Your Money…Without Even Realizing It," 2020, https://wisemoneywomen.com/7-signs-your-failing-at-managing-your-money-without-even-realizing-it/

30. "Why Have a Code of Conduct," https://www.ethics.org/resources/free-toolkit/code-of-conduct/

31. "Code of Conduct," https://www.ganintegrity.com/compliance-glossary/code-of-conduct/

32. "Using a Code of Conduct to Build Trust in the Workplace," 2011, https://www.workplaceethicsadvice.com/2011/10/using-a-code-of-conduct-to-build-trust-in-the-workplace.html

33. Jocelyn Stange, "How to Improve Employee Retention: 5 Ways to Keep Your Employees," 2021, https://www.quantumworkplace.com/future-of-work/how-to-improve-employee-retention

34. Lesley Vallance, "20 tips for maintaining a healthy work-life balance," 2020, https://www.linkedin.com/pulse/20-tips-maintaining-healthy-work-life-balance-lesley-vallance/

35. Deborah Jian Lee, "6 Tips For Better Work-Life Balance," 2014, https://www.forbes.com/sites/deborahlee/2014/10/20/6-tips-for-better-work-life-balance/?sh=84f563429ff5

36. Rieva Lesonsky, "10 Ways to Get New Customers," 2017, https://www.sba.gov/blog/10-ways-get-new-customers

37. Rebecca Patterson, "Seven Ways To Identify, Your Ideal Client," 2020, https://www.forbes.com/sites/forbescoachescouncil/2020/04/17/seven-ways-to-identify-your-ideal-client/?sh=582334e44c21

38. "Top 3 Reasons Why Beauty Salons Fail," https://salonbusiness-boss.com/top-3-reasons-why-beauty-salons-fail/

39. RocketSpace, "Business Plan Checklist: 5 Components Startups Must Include," 2018, https://www.rocketspace.com/tech-startups/business-plan-checklist-5-components-startups-must-include

40. Brian O'Connell, "What Is Leverage in Finance and What Is The Formula?" 2018, https://www.thestreet.com/personal-finance/what-is-leverage-finance-14700895

41. Admin, "How to find your niche in the beauty industry," 2020, https://launchmybeautyproduct.com/2020/06/24/how-to-find-your-niche-in-the-beauty-industry/

42. Andrew Deen, "Five Signs That. It's Time to Scale up Your Business," https://articles.bplans.com/five-signs-that-its-time-to-scale-up-your-business/

43. "4 Things to Consider Before Franchising a Business,"

44. Franchise Direct, "The Benefits of Franchising: What are the Advantages to Being a Franchisee," https://www.franchisedirect.com/ultimate-guide-to-franchising/benefits-of-franchising/

45. VB Staff, "50% of Businesses Fail in Their First 5 Years, What's the Secret for Those That Survive?" 2019, https://venturebeat.com/business/50-of-businesses-fail-in-their-first-5-years-whats-the-secret-for-those-that-survive/

46. Guest Blogger, "How to Strategically Downsize Your Business," 2019, https://www.bamboohr.com/blog/how-to-strategically-downsize-your-business

Made in the USA
Columbia, SC
21 April 2023

15376766R00083